Advance Praise 1
Migration a

The authors skilfully and effectively de: *..., ... migration and development nexus that I found most revealing and enlightening. Instead they propose an alternative understanding of this nexus drawing on critical development theory. This text is an admirable addition to this multilingual book series that challenges the dominant neoliberal paradigm and its policies.*

— Cristóbal Kay, International Institute of Social Studies, The Hague

This is an exciting book dealing with one of the most important issues of the day, namely why people migrate and what impact it has on sending and receiving societies. Delgado Wise and Veltmeyer have done a great job to clarify and explain the issues involved.

— Ronaldo Munck, Head of Civic Engagement, President's Office, Dublin City University

This small book provides us with a big idea of how to critically examine the migration-development nexus from the perspective of political economy. It addresses with analytical acuity the three challenging research fields in one go, i.e., migration studies, development studies and agrarian studies.

— Jingzhong Ye, Professor of Development Studies and Dean, College of Humanities and Development Studies, China Agricultural University

Agrarian Change and Peasant Studies: Little Books on Big Issues

AGRARIAN CHANGE, MIGRATION AND DEVELOPMENT

AGRARIAN CHANGE, MIGRATION AND DEVELOPMENT

Raúl Delgado Wise
Henry Veltmeyer

AGRARIAN CHANGE AND PEASANT STUDIES SERIES

Practical Action Publishing Ltd
The Schumacher Centre, Bourton on Dunsmore, Rugby, Warwickshire, CV23 9QZ, UK
www.practicalactionpublishing.org

Published in North America by Fernwood Publishing, Canada, 2016
This edition published by Practical Action Publishing Ltd, 2016

A catalogue record for this book is available from the British Library.
A catalogue record for this book has been requested from the Library of Congress.

ISBN 978-185339--917-6 Paperback
ISBN 978-185339-916-9 Hardback
ISBN 978-178044-917-3 Ebook
ISBN 978-1-78044-916-6 Library PDF

Citation: Delgado, Raúl (2016) *Agrarian Change, Migration and Development*, Rugby, UK:
Practical Action Publishing, < http://dx.doi.org/10.3362/ 9781780449166

Since 1974, Practical Action Publishing has published and disseminated books and
information in support of international development work throughout the world. Practical
Action Publishing is a trading name of Practical Action Publishing Ltd (Company Reg.
No. 1159018), the wholly owned publishing company of Practical Action. Practical Action
Publishing trades only in support of its parent charity objectives and any profits are cov-
enanted back to Practical Action (Charity Reg. No. 247257, Group VAT Registration No.
880 9924 76).

Cover photograph: Juan García Davish. From the series: The Death's Route
Cover design by John van der Woude
Printed in the UK by 4edge Limited

Contents

Series Editors' Foreword

Agrarian Change, Migration and Development by Raúl Delgado Wise and Henry Veltmeyer is the sixth volume in the Agrarian Change and Peasant Studies Series from ICAS (Initiatives in Critical Agrarian Studies). The first volume is Henry Bernstein's *Class Dynamics of Agrarian Change*, followed by Jan Douwe van der Ploeg's *Peasants and the Art of Farming*, Philip McMichael's *Food Regimes and Agrarian Questions*, Ian Scoones' *Sustainable Livelihoods and Rural Development*, and Marc Edelman and Saturnino M. Borras Jr.'s *Politics of Transnational Agrarian Movements*. Together, these six books re-affirm the strategic importance and relevance of applying agrarian political economy analytical lenses in agrarian studies today. They suggest that succeeding volumes in the series will be just as politically relevant and scientifically rigorous.

A brief explanation of the series will help put the current volume by Delgado Wise and Veltmeyer into perspective in relation to the ICAS intellectual and political project. Today, global poverty remains a significantly rural phenomenon, with rural populations comprising three-quarters of the world's poor. Thus, the problem of global poverty and the multidimensional (economic, political, social, cultural, gender, environmental and so on) challenge of ending it are closely linked to rural working people's resistance to the system that continues to generate and reproduce the conditions of rural poverty and their struggles for sustainable livelihoods. A focus on rural development thus remains critical to development thinking. However, this focus does not mean de-linking rural from urban issues. The challenge is to better understand the linkages between them, partly because the pathways out of rural poverty paved by neoliberal policies and the war on global poverty engaged in and led by mainstream international financial and development institutions to a large extent simply replace rural with urban forms of poverty.

Mainstream approaches in agrarian studies are generously financed and thus have been able to dominate the production and publication of research and studies on agrarian issues. Many of the institutions (such as the World Bank) that promote this thinking have also been able to acquire skills in producing and propagating highly accessible and policy-oriented publications that are widely disseminated worldwide. Critical thinkers in leading academic institutions are able to challenge this mainstream approach, but they are generally confined to academic circles with limited popular reach and impact.

There remains a significant gap in meeting the needs of academics (teachers, scholars and students), social movement activists and development practitioners in the global south and the north for scientifically rigorous yet accessible, politically relevant, policy-oriented and affordable books in critical agrarian studies. In response to this need, ICAS — in partnership with the Dutch development agency Interchurch Organization for Development Cooperation or ICCO-Cooperation — is launching this series. The idea is to publish "state of the art small books" that explain a specific development issue based on key questions, including: What are the current issues and debates in this particular topic and who are the key scholars/thinkers and actual policy practitioners? How have such positions developed over time? What are the possible future trajectories? What are the key reference materials? And why and how is it important for NGO professionals, social movement activists, official development aid circles and nongovernmental donor agencies, students, academics, researchers and policy experts to critically engage with the key points explained in the book? Each book combines theoretical and policy-oriented discussion with empirical examples from different national and local settings.

The series will be available in multiple languages in addition to English, starting with Chinese, Spanish, Portuguese, Bahasa, Thai and Russian. The Chinese edition is in partnership with the College of Humanities and Development of the China Agricultural University in Beijing, coordinated by Ye Jingzhong; the Spanish edition with the PhD Programme in Development Studies at the Autonomous University of Zacatecas in Mexico, coordinated by Raúl Delgado Wise, HEGOA Institute (Basque Public University), coordinated by Gonzalo Fernándes, and EHNE Bizkaia, coordinated by Xarles Iturbe, both in the Basque country; the Portuguese edition with the Universidade Estadual Paulista, Presidente Prudente (UNESP) in Brazil, coordinated by Bernardo Mançano Fernandes, and the Universidade Federal do Rio Grande do Sul (UFRGS) in Brazil, coordinated by Sergio Schneider; the Bahasa edition with University of Gadjah Mada in Indonesia, coordinated by Laksmi Savitri; the Thai edition with RCSD of University of Chiang Mai, coordinated by Chayan Vaddhanaphuti; and the Russian edition with the Russian Presidential Academy of National Economy and Public Administration (RANEPA), coordinated by Teodor Shanin and Alexander Nikulin.

Given the objectives of the Agrarian Change and Peasant Studies Series, one can easily understand why we are delighted to have as Book 6 the work by Delgado Wise and Veltmeyer. The first six volumes fit together well in terms of themes, accessibility, relevance and rigour. We are excited about the bright future of this important series!

Saturnino M. Borras Jr., Max Spoor and Henry Veltmeyer
ICAS Book Series Editors

Interchurch Organization for Development Cooperation Statement

The Interchurch Organization for Development Cooperation (ICCO) has partnered with ICAS to produce the Book Series on Agrarian Change and Peasant Studies.

ICCO works for a just world without poverty — a world where people can claim and assume their rights in a sustainable society. Key principles are secure and sustainable livelihoods and justice and dignity for all. Sustainable agriculture and food systems are key to realizing this vision. ICCO, together with ICAS, acknowledges that the current mainstream thinking about the rural world will not lead to sustainable alternatives to agrarian systems that contribute to hunger, malnutrition, violations of rights (right to food and other human rights) and unsustainable use of soils and water leading to pollution and loss of biodiversity. ICCO acknowledges that more research and exchange among scholars, practitioners and policymakers is badly needed to find answers. Answers, not just one answer. The world cannot afford anymore to simplify problems in order to develop a "one size fits all" solution leading to a silver bullet that tends to miss the target. We need a plurality of solutions adapted to local contexts and that fuel the thinking of a diverse range of policymakers, activists and other actors in several sectors. We need diverse inputs from a broad range of people who suffer from hunger, who are kicked off their land and yet have ideas and energy to improve their livelihoods and realize their human rights.

What follows is the type of agrarian system ICCO supports in order to contribute to the realization of this vision: ICCO promotes agriculture that locally feeds people, strives to add value locally and is environmentally sustainable. It promotes an agricultural system in which people are central and that allows for self-determination, empowerment and governance of farmers themselves, but also in negotiation with consumers. This agricultural system allows male and female farmers to organize themselves according to their own needs and to make their own choices. It sustainably builds on the characteristics of the local environment (soil, water, biodiversity). We also know that agricultural systems are bound with other sectors and cannot survive in isolation: we see rural-urban (re)migration and we see trade and markets. Above all we see people living in rural settings that should be able to determine their own choices, supported by a favourable (political, social and economic) environment.

To make this happen, stable, reliable and just access to and control over productive resources such as water, land and genetic material such as seeds and tubers are essential. Related to this, but also in a broader context, ICCO supports small-scale producers' involvement in decision-making about their livelihoods and works for more equal power relations in and between agricultural and other systems. ICCO Cooperation acknowledges the interrelatedness between the agricultural and food systems in the global north and south and acknowledges that these linkages, as well as power imbalances, need to be challenged in order to be able to sustainably feed the world.

This type of alternative agrarian systems is knowledge-intensive. We need more research that is relevant to support and stimulate the further development of this type of agricultural system and promote pro-poor agrarian change. ICCO is looking for and working towards justice, democracy and diversity in agrarian and food systems. In order to make this happen, analytical tools and frameworks are necessary for informed collective action and advocacy work. It is in this context that we find the ICAS Book Series of great importance to ICCO, its partners worldwide and to broader audiences.

Utrecht, The Netherlands

Acknowledgements

The authors would like to acknowledge in particular the enormous and substantive contributions of Errol Sharpe, the publisher of Fernwood Publishing, not only to the production of this book but more generally to the overall project of producing a series of small books on big issues related to agrarian change and development. Errol accompanied the editors from the outset in their conception of ICAS, and his enthusiastic support and encouragement—and of course, his commitment to publish the series—were vital not just for originating and nurturing the project but for the evident success of the project: it has exceeded our expectations.

The authors would also like to acknowledge the support of the editors and their collaborators in the ICAS network, as well as the excellent translation of this book by Igor Ampuero, a pivotal member of the CDS network in Bolivia who not only produced an excellent translation but did so in the spirit of solidarity with the project.

The authors also wish to acknowledge the superb copyediting of the manuscript by Brenda Conroy. It is amazing to us that what we had thought to be a reasonably well-written text turned out to have all sorts of glitches and much in need of a thoroughly professional editing.

Finally, the authors would like to acknowledge the contributions of other members of both the International Migration and Development network (RIMD) and the Critical Development Studies (CDS) network, both of them housed in the Development Studies program of Universidad Autónoma de Zacatecas. The critical thinking manifest in this book reflects a vision and ideas about alternative forms and paths of development that have been nurtured by both of these networks.

Introduction

Between 1970 and 2012 the number of international migrants worldwide more than doubled, from 84 million to 232 million. In 1970, about one out of every 29 people lived in a country where international migrants composed a tenth or more of the total population. Four decades later, the ratio was nearly one in nine (Terrazas 2011: 1). Much of this growth took the form of mass migration from poor countries in the global south, on the periphery of the world capitalist system, to the wealthier countries in the global north. While in earlier periods of capitalist development people also migrated for economic reasons, motivated by a desire for a better life and a search for more opportunity, the largest flow of migrant labour was from the European centre of world capitalism to European "white" settlements in the North American outposts of the British Empire. But in the current conjuncture of capitalist development (the neoliberal era), most migration is in a south-north/south-south direction. Within the migrant-receiving countries in the north, these migrants generally settle in the larger cities, urban gateways to an apparently modern style of life and hoped-for economic opportunity.

International migration as an increasingly visible global phenomenon in recent decades has led to a voluminous academic literature and numerous official reports exploring such questions as:

1. What are the origins and motivations of migrants for leaving their countries of origin to seek opportunities abroad?
2. What are the root causes and objectively given conditions — the driving forces — of the migration process?
3. What are the social dimensions of the migration process regarding the social composition of labour migration streams and flows, the migration-development nexus, and the impact of migration on societies and communities in both the country of origin and in the destination country?
4. What are the macroeconomic and micro-social benefits of migration to the receiving and sending countries? And what are

the associated costs? Who receives the benefits and who bear the costs?

5. What is the relationship between migration and development in the migrant's country of origin and the destination?

6. What is the role of the state in regulating or managing the international flows of migrant workers?

7. How does migration further the process of capital accumulation under neoliberal capitalism dominated by monopoly capital?

8. Why is neoliberal capitalism adverse to the free movement of persons while capitalism in earlier periods encouraged international migration?

As for the first two questions the literature places migrants into the following three basic categories: *economic migrants* — a large stream of individuals in search for a better way of life and greater economic opportunities, and those seeking refuge from poverty or oppressive socioeconomic conditions; *environmental refugees* — those seeking to escape environmental degradation and natural disaster (drought, floods, climate change, etc.); and *political refugees* — those seeking to escape conditions of political conflict, insecurity, persecution or oppression.

In contrast with the vast literature on international migration, studies on internal migration have been relegated to second place, particularly in the realm of contemporary capitalism, namely neoliberal globalization. But it should be understood that in this context there are close links between internal and international migration. The number of internal (mostly rural-urban) migrants has been estimated at 750 million (IOM 2014), which, together with international migrants, add up to nearly one billion over the course of the decades-long neoliberal era. Considering that most migrants are labour migrants, nearly one of every three workers in the world lives in a place different from where they were born. In most cases they constitute a highly vulnerable segment of the working class, often subjected to discrimination and conditions of super-exploitation.

Regarding the economic category of migrants — the central concern of this book — the literature divides them into two groups: those who choose to migrate in the search for better economic conditions and those who we might term "economic refugees," driven to migrate from their communities and way of life by extreme poverty, conditions such as deprivation, social exclusion and lack of economic opportunity. The decision to migrate, often at great personal cost to the migrant, is explained in terms of some combination of push and pull factors.[1] However, we look at the question from a political economy perspective,[2] arguing that, while the search for economic opportunities exerts a powerful pull, there is little question that the vast majority of economic migrants and migrant workers migrate not by choice but in response to the limiting or oppressive conditions created by the workings of the capitalism, particularly in their home countries as a result of the upsurge of uneven development. While a majority of migration scholars might cite the desire to escape poverty, or relative disparities in the economic development of migrant sending and receiving countries,[3] as an explanation of the motivation to migrate, they do not blame the forces of capitalist development for this poverty. In fact, they see capitalism as the solution.

There is little question and few studies about the system dynamics of migrant labour — the dominant role of capitalism in generating the forces that lead to and therefore can be used to explain the massive flows of international migrants in the world today. The vast volume of writings in the mainstream tradition of migration studies focus exclusively on questions 1–6, ignoring 7–8. These studies, conducted predominantly by neoclassical economists, anthropologists and sociologists, are concerned almost entirely with the motivations of migrants who are assumed to freely choose to migrate. Yet structural conditions and system dynamics in a very real sense condition and even force these individuals, and betimes entire families, to migrate. The issue here is free choice or forced migration? Do these migrants have a choice? What are their options? The fundamental concern in the social scientific study of migration is to explain the strategic and structural conditions that drive the decisions of individuals and families to migrate and the consequences of these decisions for the migrants themselves as well as for the societies of origin, transit and destination.

The methods of analysis used in these studies can also be placed into two categories. First, the method used predominantly by writers in the mainstream of migration studies is to search for correlations and relations of cause between two sets of social facts[4] — the decision to migrate (the dependent variable in the explanation) and the objectively given and/or subjective conditions, the presence or absence of which is correlated with the decision to migrate and thus deemed to be the "independent variable," or explanatory factors. The explanatory factors in this analysis are viewed as conditions that either "push" individuals to act in a certain way, or that exert a powerful "pull." However, an alternative political economy tradition of migration studies explains the underlying motivation to migrate — in many if not all cases forced — in terms of the structure and dynamics of the operating capitalist system. This system can be defined in terms of the mode of production, i.e., a particular combination of the existing forces of production and the corresponding relations of production and the main trend inherent in those relations toward uneven development.

From this political economy, or Marxist, perspective, the focus of this book is on what might be described as the labour migration dynamics of the capitalist development process, or the migration-development nexus. At issue in this development process — the development of society's forces of production and corresponding social relations — is the capital-labour relation, which constitutes the economic base of the social structure in all capitalist societies, as well as the structure formed by a global division in the wealth of nations. The first has to do with two basic social classes: the capitalist class, membership in which can be defined in terms of a relation of property in the means of production; and the working class, whose labour power is the fundamental source of value — the value of commodities that are bought and sold on the market, and which can be measured in terms of hours of work under given social and technological conditions[5] — and surplus value or profit, the driving force of capitalist development.

Marx's theory of capitalist development, which remains the only useful tool for decoding the structural dynamics of the capitalist system in its evolution and development of the forces of production, is constructed around four fundamental propositions:

1. that labour is the source of value (the labour theory of value);
2. that wage labour is a hidden mechanism of economic exploitation (extraction of surplus value from the direct producer or worker by paying workers less than the actual or total value produced);
3. that capitalism has an inherent propensity towards crisis (viz., Marx's theory that specifies a tendency for a fall in the average rate of profits); and
4. what Marx described as "the general law of capital accumulation," which specifies a two-fold tendency, on the one hand, towards the centralization and concentration of capital and, on the other, towards the "multiplication of the proletariat" — the transformation of a class of small landholding agricultural producers (family or peasant farmers) into a proletariat of wage labourers and an industrial reserve army of surplus rural and urban labour.

We elaborate on proposition #4 in Chapter 1. From a political economy and critical agrarian studies perspective, it provides a framework for understanding the dynamics of internal and international migration today.

Methodological Individualism versus Class Analysis

A key presupposition of the approach used in this book to analyze the dynamics of migration and capitalist development is that individuals act, and respond to the forces operating on them, not as individuals but as members of a social class that is formed in the process of production. This means, among other things, that analysis should not abstract individuals from the social context in which they are embedded. Such abstraction — what we might term "methodological individualism" — is central to economics in the liberal tradition — classical theory, social liberalism (as it is constituted within the framework of development economics and the concept of "human development"[6]) and neoliberalism, with reference to the fundamental ideas shared by members of the thought collective formed by Von Hayek in the 1930s (Mirowski and Plehwe 2009). These ideas serve as the theoretical foundation of the "new economic model" (neoliberalism, free market capitalism) that was constructed — in Latin America at any rate — and widely implemented in the 1980s in the form of the Washington Consensus (Williamson 1990). In this economistic way of thinking, people are viewed not as members of a social group, but as individuals, each of whom in their economic transactions makes a rational calculation of self-interest, choosing a course of action that maximizes this interest. On the basis of this assumption, development economists have constructed a widely used methodology in which individuals are grouped with others according to their share of the national income, reducing them to a statistical category. This type of analysis allows economists to approximate the social condition of each individual in the distribution of national production (their share of the social product) by sorting them into statistical groups — deciles or quintiles of income earners. The problem with this method of income class analysis is that in the real world individuals do not "act" as members of a statistical group (as part of the bottom or top class of income earners, for example); rather, they act in terms of conditions that they share with other members of the group, community or society to which they belong. That is, an individual's social or class consciousness — an awareness of their social or class position and relation to others in the groups or society they belong to — is a critical factor of social or political action.

In contrast to the individualistic approach used by most economists, Karl Marx, among others, argued that individuals, like markets (as argued by Karl Polanyi in his book *The Great Transformation*), are embedded in "society" and cannot be properly understood outside the social relations of production, relations that they necessarily enter into early on. Accordingly, Marx classified individuals according their relation to production or their social class, i.e., the conditions of their social existence determined by the prevalent mode of production. He theorized that at each stage in the evolution of society's forces of production there is formed a corresponding structure of production relations, and thus that capitalist society is based on the capital-labour relation. This specifies the existence of two basic classes: the bourgeoisie, or the capitalist class, which exists in a relation of private property to the means of production; and the working class, those who, by virtue of being dispossessed from their means of production, are compelled to exchange their labour power for a living wage in the labour market.

Studies on migration and development deploy four different methods of class analysis, each associated with a different way of theorizing the migration-development nexus: (1) occupational class analysis, which defines individuals according to the work they do; (2) income class analysis, which groups individuals or households into deciles or quintiles of income earners to determine their percentile share of national income; (3) social class analysis, which looks at the individual's relationship to the market, or their capacity for material consumption, and thus their "life chances"; and (4) political economy analysis — the method used in this book — which determines the individual's relation to production and the objective and social conditions of this relation.[7]

Organization of the Book

At issue in this book are the development and migration dynamics associated with the evolution of the world capitalist system. But these dynamics include complex issues that are necessarily excluded from consideration. These issues relate to what might be described as the "refugee problem" — the forced migration of hundreds of millions of people due to conditions generated by a growing ecological crisis of global proportions and spreading political conflicts and "wars" — wars over natural resources and wars waged by diverse social groups to gain control over the instruments of state power. This book is not concerned with these issues but rather with issues related to the development dynamics of migrant labour.

The book begins with an overview of different ways of understanding and analyzing the development dynamics of internal and international migration. Four different theoretical and methodological approaches, and associated analytical frameworks and theoretical propositions, are identified and discussed. We argue that the most useful approach is based on what is described as the "political economy of development," which is informed by a Marxist theory of capitalist development, a theory that seeks to explain the fundamental dynamics of social change and economic development in terms of the workings and evolution of the capitalist system. In the context of contemporary capitalism, i.e., capitalism in an era of neoliberal globalization, a system dominated by monopoly capital, what is the role of migration? That is, how does migration further the process of capital accumulation under neoliberal capitalism? How is migration in this context harnessed so as to stimulate capital accumulation?[8]

The second chapter provides the framework for our analysis of the dynamics of internal (rural-urban) migration in the global south and international (south-north) migration. As we see it these dynamics are rooted in the structure and evolution of capitalism as a world system. The origins of this system has been and is still surrounded by debate and controversy, but there is no question about the central importance of what Marx described as "primitive accumulation," the essential feature of which is the separation of the direct agricultural producers, or small landholding family farmers or peasants, from the land and their means of production.

The complex dynamics of this process, and the subsequent development of the available forces of production — capitalist development — put into motion forces that have resulted in a process of productive and social transformation that, on the one hand, has led to an unprecedented increase (albeit very uneven) in the wealth of nations, but on the other hand, has created conditions that threaten the livelihoods and well-being of working people across the world, even the very survival of the human species.

The chapter provides an analysis of these contradictory forces of capitalist development as they relate to what is widely understood, and has been debated as, the "agrarian question" — the productive and social transformation of an agriculture-based society and economy into a modern industrial capitalist system with all of its contradictions. On the class dynamics of agrarian change see Bernstein (2012).

Chapter 3 delves into the complex dynamics of three interrelated processes: (1) capitalist development of the forces of production and the relations of production that correspond to different phases in this development; (2) the capitalist labour process — the social production process of transforming an idea related to a need or problem, raw materials and human labour into commodities to be bought and sold on the market; and (3) economic and social development — a process resulting from a project and related efforts to bring about an improvement in the social condition of a given population or people, and to build the institutional and policy framework for bringing about the changes needed for this improvement.

As in the case of the "agrarian question," addressed in Chapter 2 regarding the capitalist development of agriculture, or the transition towards capitalism, the evolution of capitalism as a world system raises fundamental questions about the role of migration in the development process. While Chapter 2 focuses on the dynamic of internal (rural-urban) migration associated with, or resulting from, the capitalist development of agriculture, Chapter 3 analyzes the dynamics of international migration within the institutional and policy framework of the world capitalist system.[9]

The chapter addresses three principal themes. The first is that most migrant workers today are still locked into forms of labour exploitation that marked the birth of global capitalism. Second, the search by capitalists at the centre of the world system for cheap labour has brought about a new international division of labour and has dramatically expanded international flows of migrant workers in a south-north direction. The chapter analyses the dynamics of international migration in the context of the world capitalist system and the project of international development, which is designed fundamentally as a means of ensuring the stability and survival of capitalism. The third theme relates to the role of governments in the imperialist state system in controlling the flow of and policing international migration, i.e., harnessing the international flow of migrant workers to the national interest defended and advanced by these countries, an interest that is generally equated with the interests of capital in securing a labour force for its national and global operations.

In Chapter 4 we turn to the international dynamics of labour migration. These dynamics include formation of an international division of labour and a global labour market that reflects both national differences in wage rates and working conditions, and the workings of market forces and migration policies. From a discussion of the dynamics the chapter turns to the system of global labour arbitrage used as a means of restructuring global production, commerce and services by taking advantage of the extraordinary availability of cheap and flexible labour in the global south. This has been functional for monopolizing the process of knowledge production, the development of a south-north brain drain, and the restructuring of the global labour market under a neoliberal policy regime.

This neoliberal restructuring process, which in Latin America has taken the form of "structural reform" in the direction of free market capitalism,[10] includes: (1) the reinforcement of migration processes as mechanisms of accumulation; (2) creation of a dispersed and vulnerable proletariat available to global networks of monopoly capital; (3) the covert proletarianization of highly qualified scientific and technological workers; (4) the real and disguised proletarianization of the peasantry; (5) the semi-proletarianization of migrant workers; (6) the expansion of the reserve army of labour; and (7) the subordination and resistance of the intellectual worker.

In Chapter 5 we turn to the sociology of migration with reference to its social dimension and the underside of development — the social cost of the migration process borne by the migrants themselves as they choose or are forced to relocate from their communities in the countryside to the urban centres and cities of the contemporary capitalist world system. There are multiple social dimensions of the migration-development problematic. In this chapter we can only hint at the complexity of the problem by focusing on four particular issues: (1) the gender dimension of the development-migration process; (2) the negative social impact of this process on migrant-sending communities regarding the loss of their most economically productive members; (3) the social costs borne by migrant families in terms of forced separation (migrants having to travel by themselves and leave behind parents, spouses and children), vulnerability and exposure to conditions of personal insecurity and exploitation; and (4) the experience of child migrants, large numbers of whom are forced to undertake the tortuous migration journey by themselves in the concern and need to join their parents.

In conclusion, Chapter 6 examines diverse dimensions of the migration-development nexus and advances ideas for a new theoretical approach towards understanding its dynamics. The point of departure here is the way that international organizations such as the World Bank link migration and development. In various ways these organizations see remittances, as well as the "circulation of brain-power," as tools for the development of the poor migrant-sending underdeveloped countries.

The chapter argues that this idea of the role of migrant remittances is part of a mythology designed to obscure the root causes of current labour migration dynamics. We identify five particular elements of this mythology, which serves as a convenient ideological cover for the construction of public policy regarding migration.

Deconstruction of this mythology, which surrounds the question of migration and development, leads to an entirely different perspective, one that emphasizes both the structural and the strategic dimensions of migration from a political economy and critical development perspective. From this perspective analysis of the migration-development nexus takes into account not only the workings of the capitalist system in the current conjuncture of the development process but also interrelated issues such as social agency, the global context, regional integration, the role of the nation-state and the intra-national dimension of development.

As for policymakers in the area it is suggested that migrant-sending countries should adopt policies designed to protect local populations from the destructive forces of capitalist development, forces that compel large numbers to migrate and that promote a process of endogenous development in peripheral regions and underdeveloped countries. It is also suggested that both migrant-sending and migrant-receiving countries be more cognizant of the structural development constraints placed on the former and that these countries be compensated for the contributions that migrants in both high- and lower-skilled migration streams make to the migrant-receiving countries. In addition, the development potential of migration can be increased by creating more effective legal channels for high- and lower-skilled migration and integration policies that favour the socioeconomic mobility of migrants and avoid their marginalization (de Haas 2012).

Notes

1. Reference to push and pull factors does not imply our adherence to its most common usage, where a list of factors without any hierarchical order is given. It is crucial to dialectally distinguish between structural and individual factors, with particular reference to the main and the secondary contradictions involved in the migration process.

2. Political economy is fundamentally concerned with and focused on what might be described as "structural factors," with reference to conditions that, as Karl Marx argued as a matter of principle, are "objective" in their effects on people according to their location in the class structure of the economic system and the forces generated by the workings of this system. Needless to say, there is also a subjective dimension to the dynamics of capitalist development. The "subjective" has to do with how individuals experience and react to (interpret) the structural forces that operate on them and constrain their options and responses — and in the context of our analysis — force or motivate them to migrate. This political economy perspective on migration is supplemented with a sociological perspective on the social dimensions of the migration processes (Chapter 5).

3. This is indeed the accepted explanation of the motivation to migrate given by Dhananjayan Srisjkandarajah, a leading researcher at the Institute for Public Policy Research, in a study commissioned by the Global Commission on International Migration. Although she is careful not to attribute her analysis to the GGIM, there is no doubt that it represents a widely held view on what the author describes as the "migration-development-migration" nexus.

4. "Social facts" in this methodological context ("positivism," as established by the classical sociological theorist Emile Durkheim) refer to conditions that are "external to individuals" and "coercive in their effects" on them.

5. On the presumption that the worker's labour power was a commodity like any other and that therefore its value was determined by calculating the socially necessary labour time expended in the production of this commodity, Marx theorized that labour was the fundamental source of surplus value; that labour power is the only commodity able to produce value greater than itself (surplus value), which is extracted by the capitalist from the worker by paying the worker a wage that represents the value of labour power rather than surplus value. This theory is generally regarded as Marx's greatest theoretical contribution — the discovery that the wage relation between capital and labour discloses the "inner secret" of capitalism: that wage labour is the fundamental mechanism of surplus extraction or exploitation, the source of profit.

6. On the concept of human development, and the liberal reformist ap-

proach to development on which it is based, see, inter alia, Haq (1995), Sen (1999), Jolly, Stewart and Mehrotra (2000). For a critical reflection on this approach see Chapter 1 of Veltmeyer (2014).

7. For an application of this method to an analysis of the dynamics of agrarian change see Bernstein (2012).

8. From this political economy and critical development studies perspective, what neoliberal theorists regard as the development impact of migration is really about the migration dynamics of capital accumulation. As Canterbury (2012: 1) has it: "Each epoch of capitalism, dominated by a given class of capitalist, produces its own migration dynamics including arrangements for capital accumulation from migration processes. In the same manner that mercantile and industrial capitalists created elaborate processes to stimulate and exploit migrant labour in order to accumulate capital, neoliberal capital is exploiting migration processes to accumulate capital in the neoliberal epoch of capitalism."

9. Our use of the term "world capitalist system" does not mean that we subscribe to "world systems theory," elaborated by Immanuel Wallerstein and colleagues at the University of New York at Binghampton and the Fernand Braudel Center. On the contrary, we subscribe to a historical materialist approach to a class analysis of the long-term dynamics of social change, and the theory of capital and capitalist development elaborated by Karl Marx. This theory relates to both the geoeconomics of capital (capitalism) and the geopolitics of capital (imperialism).

10. On this neoliberal restructuring process see, inter alia, Petras and Veltmeyer (2001).

References

Bernstein, Henry. 2012. *Class Dynamics of Agrarian Change.* Halifax: Fernwood Publishing.

Canterbury, D. 2012. *Capital Accumulation and Migration.* Leiden: Brill.

De Haas, Hein. 2012. "The Migration and Development Pendulum: A Critical View on Research and Policy." *International Migration* 50, 3: 8–25.

Haq, Mahbub Ul. 1995. *Reflections on Human Development.* New York: Oxford University Press.

IOM (International Organization for Migration). 2014. *Global Migration Trends: An Overview.* Geneva: IOM.

Jolly, Richard, Frances Stewart and Santosh Mehrotra (eds.). 2000. *Development with a Human Face: Experiences in Social Achievement and Economic Growth.* New York: Oxford University Press.

Mirowski, Philip, and Dieter Plehwe (eds.). 2009. *The Road from Mont Pelerin: The Making of the Neoliberal Thought Collective.* Cambridge: Harvard University Press.

Petras, James, and Henry Veltmeyer. 2001. *Globalization Unmasked*. Halifax: Fernwood Publications.

Sen, Amartya. 1999. *Development As Freedom*. NY: Alfred A. Knopf.

Terrazas, Aaron. 2011. "Migration and Development: Policy Perspectives from the United States." MPI *Report*, June. Migration Policy Institute.

Veltmeyer, Henry. 2014. *Human Development: Lessons from the Cuban Revolution*. Halifax: Fernwood Publishing.

Williamson, John (ed.) 1990. *Latin American Readjustment: How Much Has Happened*, Washington, DC: Institute for International Economics

Chapter 1

Rethinking Migration
in the Neoliberal Era

There are five basic theoretical and methodological approaches to understanding the migration-development nexus, each associated with a theory regarding the development dynamics of migration.

One approach — *positivism* (as it is known in social science discourse) — is used by many migration economists but can be traced back to the sociologist Emile Durkheim. It is to search for and establish a correlation between the decisions made and actions taken by individual migrants and the objectively given conditions of these decisions and actions. In this approach the underlying motivation and decision to migrate are explained in terms of the "social facts" (conditions that are external to individuals and coercive in their effects) — a combination of "push" and "pull" factors. An example of this approach can be found in a study by Dana Rowlands (2004) on the impact of poverty and environmental degradation on south-north migration flows, and the gender dimension of these flows. Typically, as in this study, there is no reference to any system dynamics.

A second approach — *constructivism* — (used by many sociologists) — seeks to take into account subjective factors such as motivation and social awareness (subjective interpretations by individuals of their own reality), which are manifest not in theoretical or political discourse but in the migrant's own words and thoughts. This approach is exemplified in a study by Tsafack and Calkins (2004), which reports on the changed socioeconomic status of migrants, as well as gender relations and the gender composition of migrant streams, but focuses on the subjective dimension of the decisions taken by particular individuals to migrate. These decisions are explained, not in terms of conditions that are "external to individuals and coercive in their effects" — conditions rooted in the economic or social structure of society — but in terms of an individual's social consciousness. In this study, and others of this genre, decisions of an individual or family to migrate are understood in terms of reports given by the migrants themselves.

A third approach to labour migration is based on an *orthodox neoclassical theory of international trade*, although as Nayyar (1994: 31–38) reminds us, this theory is mostly about the movement of goods and not very much about the movement of capital or labour across national boundaries. Insofar as exponents of this neoclassical trade theory concern themselves with international factor movements, the focus is almost exclusively on capital mobility, with labour mobility, at best, a corollary and at worst totally ignored.

Orthodox trade theory starts from David Ricardo's notion of "comparative advantage," which seeks to explain the pattern of trade between countries in terms of differences in factor endowments. In the conventional two-country–commodity-factor model used to construct this theory, the labour-abundant country's export of labour-intensive goods constitutes a "virtual" export of labour, while the capital-abundant country's export of capital-intensive goods is an implicit (but again not actual) export of capital. However, if instead of goods, one were to think of factors of production moving from countries where they are relatively abundant to where they are relatively scarce, the basis for trade in goods would narrow and vanish over time. Therefore, theoretically, the movement of capital from rich to poor countries and the movement of labour from poor to rich countries are perfectly substitutable. This approach has proven to be overly abstract and rather fruitless in terms of guiding empirical research into migration and development dynamics.

A more productive approach, which the authors of this book use, is to analyze the motivations underlying the decision to migrate in terms of conditions and forces generated in the capitalist development process, i.e., the political economy of national and international development viewed from a critical perspective (critical development studies, in the discourse of this *political economy approach*). Within this framework the fundamental concern is with the structural dynamics of labour migration and the capital-labour relation in the capitalist development process. The assumption is that the dynamics of labour migration are intimately related to the evolution of capitalism as an economic and social system.

Fifth, the *gender and development approach* to understanding and analyzing the dynamics of intra- and international migration is focused on the gender dimensions of migration. One of the most striking features of migration research over the past decade is a growing concern with the gender dimensions of the migration and capitalist development processes. This concern in part reflects the emergence of feminism in the 1980s and the centrality of gender in the study of development and development practice.[1] However, it also reflects the emergence of a women-centred approach towards migration in academe and the dissemination of a series of global reports published by a number of international organizations within the U.N. system.[2] This change in focus, according to Piper (2005) reflects two important events: (i) scholars have succeeded in bringing female migration out of the shadows in many disciplines; (ii) migration is now viewed as a gendered phenomenon that requires more sophisticated theoretical and analytical tools than sex (gender) as a dichotomous variable. Theoretical formulations of gender as relational, and as spatially and temporally contextual, have begun to inform gendered analyses of migration (Donato et al. 2006).[3]

The identification of the gender ramifications of migratory processes has resulted in greater attention paid by policymakers and scholars alike than hitherto. There are a number of reasons why it is important to understand the economic and social ramifications of migratory processes. Among these, gender differentiated population movements deserve particular attention because they act like a mirror for the way in which gender divisions of labour are incorporated into spatially uneven processes of economic development. In addition, an analysis based on gender highlights the social dimensions of migration. On the other hand, these cross-border movements – whether by women/men on their own or jointly with their spouses – have the potential to reconfigure gender relations and power inequalities. Migration can provide new opportunities for women and men to improve their lives, escape oppressive social relations and support those who are left behind. But it can also expose people to new vulnerabilities as the result of their precarious legal status, abusive working conditions, exposure to certain health risks, etc. (UNRISD 2005).

As pointed out by Piper (2005) in her review (*Gender and Migration*) for the Global Commission on International Migration, when migration involves economic betterment for the individual concerned — obtaining a job in another country and earning a wage that may be much higher in real terms than what was available at home — the successful migrant may be subject to deep gender, ethnic and racial discrimination in the host country. Although the bulk of both female and male labour migrants occupy the lowest jobs in the hierarchy of work in the destination countries due to their migration status and skill level, gender inequalities frequently combine with those of race/ethnicity and of being a non-national to make many migrant women triply disadvantaged and most likely to be over-represented in marginal, unregulated and poorly paid jobs.

Furthermore — although this applies to men as well as women, albeit less so — qualifications may not be recognized, skills may be eroded by working in jobs that are below acquired skill levels, access to social rights may be heavily constrained, and the migrant may be subject to sexual and racial harassment. At the same time several studies have explored the *contradictory* class positioning in which some labour migrants find themselves (Piper 2005). This results from the simultaneous experience of upward and downward mobility in migration, which is not necessarily the same for men and women. Discrimination, loss of status and erosion of skills in destination areas may be combined with upward mobility at home, as remittances are invested in small businesses, housing and children's education. However, women circulate differently than men and their modes of entry tend to be different, which affects their place within the labour market and access to social services. In both North America and Western Europe, where "family reunification" is an important mode of entry, migrant women often enter as wives and dependents of men who sponsor their migration, and they are usually less likely than men to be admitted on economic and humanitarian grounds. Piper notes that the effects of gender stratification do not end there. Many immigrant women engage in paid work, but like their native-born counterparts, confront a gender-stratified labour market in which they frequently find themselves at or near the bottom. Also, legal residency, gender and race all can be used as stratifying, exclusionary criteria, while gender, class and race-biased policies, regulations and practices further increase the risk to migrants' human security and rights (Piper 2005: 2).

Piper concludes from her review of the literature that although policies governing the different categories of migrant workers are expressed in gender-neutral terms, in reality they affect men and women differently for three principal reasons: first, the concentration of men and women in different migratory flows based on gender segregated labour markets; second, gendered socioeconomic power structures; and finally, sociocultural definitions of appropriate roles in the origin as well as destination countries.

The Migration-Development Nexus

Within the framework of these alternative approaches, diverse theories have been elaborated in regard to the dynamics of both internal/ international migration and the migration-development nexus. The most widely disseminated theory, *modernization,* is that international labour migration is an extension of the rural-urban migration dynamic; that is, it is a response to the workings of diverse push and pull factors in the development process, the major dimensions of which are *industrialization* (the transition from an agriculture-based economic system to a system based on capitalism and modern industry), *modernization* (the transition from a traditional communalist culture of social solidarity to a modern culture of achievement orientation, possessive individualism, materialism and consumerism) and *urbanization* (a demographic shift from the countryside to the cities as the locus of a modern way of life). Within the framework of this development process, potential migrants, it is argued, are subject to diverse pressures, both pro and con, that play into a final decision to migrate. Push factors include landlessness and rural poverty — the inability to make a living on the farm or in agriculture in a context of agrarian crisis. Pull factors include the prospect of economic opportunities and a more sustainable livelihood, hopes for improved social conditions and a better life for the family, and — particularly in regard to the rural youth, many of whom are unemployed or have few prospects — a modern way of life based on individual achievement, materialism and consumerism.

The major alternative to this modernization theory of migration is based on what we might term the *political economy of (capitalist) development*. From this political economy perspective, migration is seen as a conditioned response to the process of productive and social transformation brought about by the capitalist development of the forces of production. The fundamental theory is that the evolution of capitalism is predicated on the exploitation of an unlimited supply of surplus generated in a process of agrarian transformation — the capitalist development of agriculture.

The earliest theories of economic growth and development recognized that migration has consequences for living standards and well-being in both origin and destination countries, even as the earliest scholars of migration recognized that living conditions in both influence conditions to migrate. This distinction between "push" and "pull" factors has been a central feature of academic and policy discussions in the mainstream tradition of migration studies. Another feature has been a debate as to whether emigration is beneficial or detrimental to the development prospects of poor countries, or whether it tends to primarily benefit developed countries (De Haas 2008). The literature is divided on this question, although it is widely recognized that historically developed countries have substantively benefitted from and prospered because of immigration, while in many cases emigration has been a major drain on the poor sending countries, which in effect subsidize and finance (with human resources) the development of the rich countries. Not only have poor countries greatly contributed to the economic development of rich countries, by providing them highly qualified and skilled labour while assuming the reproduction costs of this labour, but as a result the poor sending countries are often deprived of their most productive human resources. In a very real sense people are exported to the benefit of both the migrating individuals and the recipient country, at a cost borne entirely by the migrant-sending countries. It is argued that a benefit that accrues to these countries of origin are the remittances sent home by migrants, which can be used to alleviate poverty and even, according to World Bank economists, be used for productive investment with development outcomes (Fajnzylber and López 2007). However, as we will see in Chapter 6, this is essentially a myth.

In the policy literature, discussions about the migration-development nexus tend to revolve around two questions: why people migrate and how migration trends evolve when sending countries prosper and living conditions improve. More recently, as pointed out by Piper (2005) and by Donato and colleagues (2006), there has been a shift towards a concern with the gender dimensions of the migration and capitalist development processes. Research into the first question is of interest primarily to immigration policymakers concerned with high demand for visas and spillover effects into illegal channels. The second body of research focuses on whether countries are better or worse off when their citizens move abroad. This research is of interest primarily to development policymakers concerned with the well-being of poor countries and to policymakers in the migrant-sending countries. The third body of research, based on a concern for understanding the gender dimensions of the migration process, serves as a guide by a number of international organizations within the U.N. system to policy and practice. The reports published by these organizations are also used by governments (particularly in the migrant-receiving countries) in their elaboration of migration policies. The growing importance of migration as an issue of national policy — in regard to refugee claims, the labour market, public perceptions and issues of national security — has stimulated the production of these reports and dramatically increased their usefulness for academic researchers, policymakers and politicians.

Individual Motivations as the "Root Cause" of Migration

The usual argument is that individuals migrate because they expect to materially improve their lives and that migration pressures diminish as countries prosper and living conditions improve. But this argument fails to capture the complexity of individual decisions and the forces at play in these decisions, forces that in a very real way determine or lead to the decisions to migrate. We argue that the decision to migrate is not voluntary but forced, i.e., individual decisions are underpinned, if not determined, by structural conditions (such as poverty) and forces that operate on these individuals, as well as policies that directly or indirectly generate or liberate these forces. In the context of these forces, individuals who "choose," or are forced, to migrate — especially the rural unemployed youth, those "who neither work nor study," might very well be "pulled" by the attractions of the city (opportunity for a better life, "modern lifestyle," etc.), but to explain the actions of individuals in terms of pull factors demonstrates a failure to understand the real forces at play or the consequences of forced migration. One of these consequences is that in underdeveloped or peripheral countries, which bear the reproduction costs of the labour force, the most dynamic and productive members of society — the young, the highly educated and the highly ambitious — continue to depart. And in many cases — ranging from Ecuador, El Salvador, Egypt and Lebanon to Mexico, Morocco and the Philippines — decades of sustained emigration have barely moderated poverty (provided a sort of safety-valve) but have not led to sustainable development or measurably reduced the outflow of migrants (Castles and Delgado Wise 2008).

Poverty and opportunity by themselves cannot explain individual decisions to migrate. Many relatively wealthy European countries have high emigration rates, although in these countries emigration rates are higher among the better-educated and better-off segments of society. For example, the median emigration rate in countries with low "human development" is below 4 percent, compared to 9 percent from countries with high levels of human development (Terrazas 2011: 6). Relatively few migrants from the poorest, most underdeveloped countries migrate to developed countries. They are more likely to migrate to the urban centres in their own country. In this context economists at the UNDP conclude that "development and migration go hand in hand" (UNDP 2009: 2).

The Migration-Development Nexus: Institutions at Issue

From the perspective of mainstream migration-and-development scholars with the Migration Policy Institute (MPI) or otherwise associated with the Global Commission on International Migration, there are three critical issues regarding the migration-development nexus, all connected, not with the workings of the system, but rather its institutional framework. The system as such, as is so often the case with mainstream migration economists, disappears or is hidden from view. The first issue, flagged in the June 2011 report by Aaron Terrazas to the MPI, is the role of income derived from migrant remittances as a potential catalyst of development.

Income and Remittances

The remittances that migrants send home are the most tangible and — according to the World Bank (2006) — the least controversial link between migration and development (Maimbo and Ratha 2005). Table 1.1 provides some idea of the magnitude of the flow of migrant remittances. As voluntary *intra-family* transfers, remittances are similar to other forms of household income in that they are used to reduce poverty, promote "human capital development," increase consumption and contribute to "asset accumulation" (Terrazas 2011: 8). As *cross-border transfers*, remittances also have implications for a country's balance of payments. Furthermore, remittances can have a number of secondary consequences to the extent that "they spill over into national and local economies, generating demand for goods and services or creating incentives for work and leisure" (8).

In this developmentalist perspective, remittances have far-reaching consequences for family welfare and, by extension, the communities and economies of underdeveloped countries in the global south. In Bolivia, Ecuador, and Mexico, remittances have become the first or second source of revenue used by governments to balance payments on their current account and a source of international currency reserves. Remittances have also turned out to be an important source of revenue for banks and other financial institutions that transfer funds to family members back home. For these and other reasons, facilitating the free flow of assets among families separated by migration has become a key objective of both development practitioners and policymakers (8). The neoliberal idea is that, as Canterbury has determined, "if the state makes it easier and cheaper for migrants to remit money, then migrants would use the formal financial system to

Table 1.1 Estimated Remittance Flows to Underdeveloped Countries (UDCs)

	2009	2010	2011	2012	2013	2014
(US$ billions)						
All UDCs	316	341	380	401	427	468
East Asia/Pacific	85	95	106	109	117	130
Latin America/ Caribbean	37	37	41	40	43	47
Middle East/ North Africa	57	58	62	62	67	73
South Asia	75	83	97	109	117	127
(Growth rate, %)						
All UDCs	-4.3	8.0	11.5	5.3	6.7	9.5
East Asia/Pacific	1.8	10.9	12.3	2.5	7.1	11.2
Latin America/ Caribbean	-11.8	0.9	7.3	0.9	7.1	10.0
Middle East/ North Africa	-6.2	20.9	6.1	14.3	5.1	5.7
South Asia	4.9	9.8	17.6	12.3	6.9	9.1

Source: World Bank 2013

do so ... [and] ... this would increase profits in the financial sector. Furthermore, the state should also look into the financial agencies already involved in money transfers to curtail any practices they may have that hinder remittance" (2010: 20).

Human Capital and Labour Markets

Many scholars in the mainstream of migration studies agree that emigration modestly raises the wages of workers who remain behind in the countries of origin, but since many migrants originate from the better-educated social strata of their home countries,[4] it may also raise the cost of the goods and services produced by these workers (Docquier, Ozden and Peri 2011). Some researchers argue that migration results in a loss of workers whose skills and expertise are already scarce in their countries of origin — a phenomenon known as "brain drain" (Bhagwati and Dellalfar 1973). Most of the discussion on this issue, from as early as the late 1960s by researchers associated with UNCTAD, have focused on technically skilled workers such a medical professionals, engineers, computer programmers and university researchers and faculty.

More recently, the earlier interest in the "brain drain," which implies a benefit to the north and a cost to the south, has been rekindled by a research program initiated by the World Bank focused on the dynamics of international migration and development. The program's first major publication, in 2006, was a study that examined the determinants and impact of migration and remittances in several underdeveloped countries. According to Bourguignon, the study "has provided the most extensive brain drain database ever produced and has since become the reference in this area" (2007: x). However, what Bourguignon fails to note is that the research generated on the basis of this data has been predominantly to negate the "brain drain" literature and provide a more optimistic perspective by viewing the issue as a two-way development process and promoting the notion of "brain gain" — that underdeveloped countries in the global south befit from a process of "brain circulation."

In cases where migrants have been educated at public cost — and this would seem to be in most if not all cases — we and other researchers argue that emigration represents a serious loss to the migrant-sending country (Albo and Ordaz Díaz 2011; Delgado Wise 2009). However, some researchers — and "most research," according to Terrazas (2011) — suggest that the remittances sent home by skilled migrants far exceed the cost of their education (Kuznetsov 2006; Nyarko 2011). This is clearly an issue that remains to be settled through further study and empirical research. But the educational and social reproduction costs of migrants for the countries of origin and their contribution to economic growth in the destination countries should be taken into consideration. For highly qualified or skilled migrants, these costs are greater than those for low-skilled migrants, and their economic contributions to host countries are much higher both in terms of productivity and, in an increasing rate, to the innovation sphere — i.e., a source of power and extraordinary profits for the large multinational corporations (MNCs) (Delgado Wise 2015). Moreover, the available evidence[5] seems to provide incontrovertible support for the view that the "brain drain" or the "circulation of brainpower" is an enormous boon to economic development in the global north rather than in the south. This is particularly clear given a systematic study showing that the wealth of the most developed nations in the world system is based on the accumulation of human capital, or knowledge and skills (UNU-IHDP 2012).

An idea of the magnitude of this problem for underdeveloped countries can be gleaned from the data provided by FLACSO Ecuador for countries not only in the Andes but the Caribbean, which continues to experience the highest rates of outmigration for all countries by migrants with a tertiary level of education — over 50 percent in many cases (Carrington and Detragiache 1998). According to this migration database, 25 percent of all Colombian migrants to the U.S. from 2006 to 2010 possessed a university degree — up from 22.4 percent in 2000 (*Andina Migrante* 2012). This migration pattern is reflected in OECD data that show that up to 72 percent of Colombian migrants living in the U.S. had either secondary or tertiary education, and of these, 28 percent had completed a program of university or advanced technical studies. Colombia in this respect is not typical, but nor is it unique. For example, in 2010 over 80 percent of Peruvian immigrants to the U.S. possessed some level of secondary or university education, and 15.3 percent were university educated. Studies by Lonzano and Gandini (2012) show a similar pattern for Mexico.

In the Caribbean the situation is worse. For example, according to World Bank data, 77 percent of Guyanese emigrants possessed a university education, while nine other countries in the English-speaking Caribbean had a similar proportion of university educated emigrants — 89.9 percent in the case of Surinam, 82.5 percent in Jamaica, 78.4 percent in Trinidad and Tobago, and, in the case of the poorest country in the entire hemisphere, Haiti, up to 81.6 percent of emigrants are university educated (Carrington and Detragiache 1998; *Andina Migrante* 2012: 7). What makes the situation in these countries so dire is that in some cases — Guyana, for example — well over 50 percent of the country's stock of university-educated workers has migrated and can be found abroad, in many cases in the U.S. and Canada. The scale of exported brainpower from the Caribbean is nothing less than astounding, with an inestimably negative impact on the productive capacity and development prospects of the countries in the region (Canterbury 2012).

Ideas, Attitudes and Behaviour

One way of assessing the impact of migration on development is through the flow of ideas, behaviour and social norms, which, in the academic literature, is frequently linked to the trend towards globalization — the global diffusion of a western culture associated with the "idea of freedom" (democracy) and also a capitalist culture of individual achievement, materialism and consumerism (Inglehart and Welzel 2005; Pieterse 2003). In these academic studies, particularly those informed by a "modernization theory" of international development, migration is often viewed as a mechanism of cultural transmission and the diffusion of values and beliefs.

The role of migrants in transferring technical know-how, values and social norms — the globalization of culture — has received a lot of attention by mainstream migration researchers and scholars (e.g., Kuznetsov 2006). A growing literature in this mainstream of migration and development thinking also explores the role of expatriates in promoting democratic governance and civil participation in their countries of origin. An example is Cuban expats living in the U.S. but actively engaged in the promotion of "democracy" back in Cuba. These emigrants/expats maintain connections back home with political groups. Needless to add, more often than not the promotional activities of these expatriates are funded by USAID and other agencies engaged in the imperial state project of "international cooperation," or foreign aid (Terrazas 2011).

The Gender Dimension of Migration

Global estimates confirm that for more than forty years after 1960, female migrants reached almost the same numbers as male migrants. In 1960, female migrants accounted for nearly 47 out of every 100 migrants living outside their country of birth. Since then, the share of female emigrants among all international migrants has been rising steadily, to reach 48 percent in 1990 and nearly 49 percent in 2000, when women migrants constituted nearly 51 percent of all migrants in the developed world and about 46 percent in the underdeveloped countries (ILO 2003: 9).

There are also qualitative differences between home-state and migrant women in the destination countries. The significant increases in female labour-force participation of home-state women across the OECD countries, as well as in certain destination countries in Southeast/East Asia (such as Hong Kong, Singapore, Taiwan) and in Latin America (e.g., Costa Rica, Argentina), has created a need for social services, especially where mothers of young children work full-time. Migrant women tend to be concentrated to a greater extent than their home-state peers in non-skilled, personal service work. Globally, most women migrants generate income through jobs which are considered unskilled and are poorly paid and often performed in the domestic/private domain or related to the expansion of the service industry — jobs that tend to be looked down upon socially and devalued economically (Piper 2005: 5).

Indicators of immigrant women's labour-market marginality include lower labour-force participation, low-status occupations and jobs, poor working conditions and low earnings. In North America, foreign-born women were the least likely of all groups, defined by birthplace and gender, to be in the formal labour force in the 1990s (Piper 2005: 8).

The migration process, Piper notes, involves three main phases: pre-departure, stay at the destination and return. Although the principal driver of international migration appears to be relative poverty, this not always or simply so. Gender discriminatory practices and attitudes in the pre-migration phase also play a significant role. Women's employment opportunities, education levels, health care and other services in their home communities are often less well advanced or provided for than in the case of men. In addition, there are often no, or only insufficient, safety nets for women who are single beyond an age at which it is expected of them to get married; this also applies for single mothers and women who are divorced, separated or widowed. For men and women, an emerging "culture of migration" that functions almost like a "rite of passage" to social recognition, as has been suggested in the case of the Philippines, is another element that pushes especially men into migration. In this sense, it is economic *and* social development that is the best long-term solution to lower the pressures that push people into migration (U.N. General Assembly 2004). From a gender perspective, sociocultural issues are important because — although clearly related to an economically weaker position — negative attitudes towards divorced, widowed, childless or single women also contribute to a stronger push into outmigration than that experienced by men (Piper 2005: 12). All of this, Piper observes, "impacts upon the level of choice that women have — as to whether to migrate at all, by which means, to which destination, and for what kind of employment." Restrictions on travel of unskilled women, as in Bangladesh, for example, seem to have the effect of restricting national development and increasing illegal flows (11–12).

As Piper notes, there is increased awareness of the important role that gender plays in international migration. This reflects the increased proportion of migrant women in all categories, along-side increased recognition by scholars and policymakers alike that women's experience of migration differs from that of men (Taran and Geronimi 2003: 10). What emerges is a highly complex picture of gendered outcomes of migration. This makes the assessment of gender equalizing and empowering experiences that migration may entail highly context-specific and closely connected to legal status, skill level, and socioeconomic and cultural background in the countries involved.

In her review of the gender-migration literature, Piper (2005: 45) concludes that "channels to achieve sociopolitical empowerment for all migrant workers, but especially women (for whom there seems to be a weaker support system available all around), need to be fostered, and nongovernmental organisations (trade unions, NGOs, human rights commissions, regional human rights courts) have an important role to play in this." Genuine empowerment, she adds, is about hav-ing meaningful institutional alternatives through which influence on policy and the normative/legal framework can be channelled at all stages of the migration process (pre-migration, stay abroad, return migration). This, Piper notes, is what policy should aim to achieve at every level (national, regional, global) — to empower migrants and reduce their socioeconomic and legal insecurities through an institutional set-up that is based upon a comprehensive rights-based approach. Migrants in general, and migrant women specifically, need to have a voice in decision-making.

Establishing a "social dialogue" system — by way of national and regional commissions comprised of all stakeholders — might be a way to go about this, Piper concludes. As she sees it, "overall, the mainstreaming of a gender and rights perspective into all migration interventions is desirable as well as the mainstreaming of migration into development interventions. Highlighting gender differences leads to a greater appreciation of not only the economic but the social dimensions of the development-migration nexus." This, she notes, would help both researchers and policymakers address the complex root causes that lead to migration and would help to maximize the benefits of migration to the individuals involved.

Systemic Dynamics of International Migration: Capitalism at Issue

A study by the French economist Thomas Piketty (2013) into the workings of the world capitalist system confirmed what Marx established, namely that inequality — *unequal development* of the forces of production and *social inequalities* in the distribution of wealth and income — are intrinsic features of capitalism, its "central contradiction." This contradiction is manifest both in the social structure of the capital-labour relation and in the economic structure of relations between nations on the north and south of what has emerged as a global divide in the wealth of nations. Both the capital-labour relation at the economic base of the capitalist system and international relations along the south-north divide are based on exploitation — the extraction of surplus value from the direct producers and the working classes.

Although it continues to be debated, the propensity of capitalism for unequal development has been well documented and analyzed from diverse theoretical perspectives, including dependency theory and world systems theory. A major issue in this debate is whether there is a tendency towards convergence or increasing disparities in global income — in the accumulated wealth or the GDP (the total value of goods and services) of different countries in the global economy. On this issue the United Nations Department of Economic and Social Affairs (UNDESA) in 2005 released a report that addressed what it termed the "inequality predicament," related to the fact that global wealth and incomes were divided so unequally as to be "grotesque." As the authors of this study saw it, this inequality was rooted in the history and social structure of capitalist societies but exacerbated by the neoliberal reforms implemented by so many countries at the behest of Washington — as a requirement and cost of admission into the globalization process of the new world order. In the words of a report released by the UNDP in 2010, which came to the same conclusion of a study published in the same year by ECLAC, there exists a "direct correspondence between the advance of globalization, neoliberalism, and the advance of poverty, social inequality and social inequity" (UNDP 2010: xv). The most "explosive contradictions," the report adds, "are given because the advance of [neoliberal] globalization marches hand in hand with the advance of poverty and social polarization." It is "undeniable," the report continues, "that the 1980s and 1990s [were] the creation of an abysmal gap between wealth and poverty" (xv).

The sustained and extraordinarily rapid growth of the Chinese economy over the past two decades, which has ostensibly lifted hundreds of millions of Chinese workers out of income poverty (i.e., providing them with wages above the World Bank's poverty line of $2.50 a day), and the reduction in the rate of poverty in some countries as a result of policies adopted under the new millennium goals concerted by the United Nations in 2000, have led some observers and analysts to argue the existence of a trend towards global income convergence — attenuation of the north-south divide in the wealth of nations. However, studies into global incomes (including Piketty 2013) point towards an increase in the social inequalities of incomes within nations and among them along a north-south divide. As a result of these growing inequalities, it is estimated that the per capita GDP of the underdeveloped countries (excluding China) is a mere 6.3 percent of the GDP per capita of the rich G8 countries (Foster, McChesney and Jonna 2011) and that the richest

1 percent of the world's population has managed to appropriate the bulk of the income generated in the process of social production and economic activity and now concentrates 40 percent of total global wealth (Davies et al. 2008).

This condition of social inequality — poverty and the growing immiseration of workers and those excluded from this capital accumulation and wealth generation process — is reflected in the mushrooming of billionaires across the world. In 1982, at the dawn of the neoliberal era, there were thirteen billionaires in the U.S., the hegemonic power in the world capitalist system. With the introduction of tax legislation that favoured the wealthy and the super rich, this number doubled by 1986, and by 1990, *Forbes* reported a staggering (at the time) total of ninety-nine individuals and families in the U.S. that each had net wealth in the billions of dollars. By 2006, with the wealthiest 1 percent of the population appropriating an estimated 90 percent of all the wealth generated between 1999 and 2006, the number of U.S. billionaires had doubled again. Capitalism had become thoroughly globalized and financialized, giving rise to a system dominated by monopoly capital[6] and what has been termed a "transnational capitalist class," with billionaires sprouting like mushrooms in excrement in some forty-seven countries. According to *Forbes*, the number of billionaires worldwide grew from 423 in 1996 to 691 in 2005. But then, in the lead-up to and the wake of the "global financial crisis, the number of billionaires grew exponentially. In 2013 *Forbes* listed 1,426 individuals with a combined net worth of $5.4 trillion" (Kroll 2013).

The extreme concentration of wealth and the associated divisions and social inequalities of class, race and gender, as well as geographic location, point to one of the most distressing aspects of the global development process: while a small group of capitalists have appropriated the lion's share of the wealth generated in the world system a large and growing part of the world's population is almost excluded from the benefits of economic growth and social development and are forced to bear the brunt of the exceedingly high social and environmental costs. Another distressing aspect of this process is the widespread dissemination of the idea that nothing can be done about it, that these inequalities are the unavoidable outcome of a system that cannot be changed. And there is considerable evidence to suggest that this is indeed the case; that social inequality and uneven development are intrinsic to capitalism; that the system is structured so as to reproduce and maintain the "structure of social inequality"; that the search for a solution to this problem — the "inequality predicament" as described by UNDESA — within the capitalist system is futile; that a solution to the problem requires abandoning the system — revolutionary transformation rather than institutional reform; and that the system itself as it evolves breeds class conflict and generates forces of resistance, a class struggle against the workings of the world capitalist system on the working classes and peoples across the world.

Conclusion

Notwithstanding the uncertain outcome of a protracted class struggle we have drawn the following conclusions from our analysis of the migration dynamics of global capitalist development. First, the root causes of both domestic and international migration should be sought and can be found in the workings of the capitalist system. Second, the driving force behind the abandonment by small landholding agricultural producers and peasant farmers of their farms and rural communities are forces released in the process of capitalist development in the agricultural sector — a process that can be traced out in diverse contexts throughout the twentieth and into the twenty-first century. Under the impact of these forces, the direct agricultural producers and peasant farmers are proletarianized to various degrees and in diverse ways, converting many of them into a reserve army of surplus labour for capital and generating a protracted class struggle for land and land reform. Third, an important feature of post–Second World War migration, particularly over the past three and a half decades, has been the huge and forced displacement of people from the so-called "economically backward" countries on the periphery of world capitalism. Although poverty, war and persecution are the factors most often cited as motivating factors, the driving force behind this mass immigration from the poor to the rich countries, particularly in the neoliberal era of capitalist development and globalization, is the grossly uneven distribution of wealth across the globe. As long as this is so — and given that it implicates the central contradiction of capitalism it is difficult to see a way out — the movement of people across international boundaries and frontiers can no more be stopped than the movement of people within each country — from the depressed areas to the economically vibrant zones.

In this book we are particularly interested in and concerned about the development implications of the dynamics of migrant labour in the neoliberal era of capitalist development. These dynamics have both an objective and a subjective dimension, the first of which is rooted in the structure of the capitalist system and the forces generated by this structure — forces that affect individuals and countries according to their location within the capitalist system.

From this perspective, with reference to what we term the political economy of migration, the motivation and the decision of individuals and families to migrate are conditioned by forces over which they have no control, which thus restrict their choices and shape if not determine their actions. From this perspective, migration, particularly as regards labour, can be conceptualized as forced.

However, there is also a subjective dimension to the migration process, which has more to do with the choices that individuals have, choices that are perhaps relatively less restricted. This relates in part to what has been described as the circulation of brainpower, or the mobility of highly qualified or skilled labour based on the accumulation of human capital or knowledge. Since the mobility of brainpower tends to be in a south-north direction, and the costs and benefits of this productive resource are unevenly distributed across the world capitalist system, there is no doubt that the dominant pattern in the mobility of brainpower can only be explained in terms of the systemic dynamics of capitalist development. Even so, there is no question that the subject or agent of this brainpower has a range of choice and freedom that is denied to members of the working class, whose decisions to migrate are essentially forced.

Notes

1. On the role of women in the development process and the gender dimension of development, see, inter alia, Ahooja Patel (2003) and Parpart and Barriteau (2000).

2. Two global reports (by the World Commission on the Social Dimension of Globalization in 2004 and the Commission on Human Security in 2003) placed migration issues firmly among their recommendations for a global policy agenda. Although not completely ignored, gender issues were not the focus of either report. By contrast, the March 2005 report "Gender Equality: Striving for Justice in an Unequal World" by the U.N. Research Institute for Social Development (UNRISD) discusses a number of subject areas from a clear gender perspective, and one chapter is devoted to the issue of work migration. In addition, there are two U.N. reports focusing on women and migration: one by the Division for the Advancement of Women (2004); and the latest World Survey on the role of women in development by the U.N. devoted to the issue of "women and international migration" (U.N. General Assembly, 2004).

3. For a detailed summary and classification of existing theoretical and analytical approaches to "gender and migration," see Carling (2005).

4. On this point, in the case of Mexico, see Delgado Wise 2015.

5. See the discussion of this issue in *Andina Migrante*, No. 13, July 2012, a bulletin of information on Andean migrations published by FLACSO Ecuador.

6. Neoliberal capitalism is a system of capital accumulation dominated by financial capital, unlike capitalism in the era of the development state (1945–80), which was dominated by industrial capital or what some term "monopoly capital." Finance capital operates (accumulates capital) in the sphere of financial institutions and capital markets (speculating or betting on changes in the price of commodities) rather than economic production. "Financial capital," writes Petras (2007), "is rapidly bringing all aspects of economy and society under its thumb. Financial capital does not have the legs to stand on its own but needs the productive economy that migrants participate in for which it has created the framework of operation." He adds that financial capital "writes the rules, controls its regulators and has secured license to speculate on everything, everywhere and all the time."

References

Ahooja Patel, Krishna. 2003. *Development Has a Woman's Face: Insights from Within the UN*. Halifax: Fernwood Publications.

Albo Adolfo, and Juan Luis Ordaz Diaz. 2011. "La Migración Mexicana hacia los Estados Unidos: Una breve radiografía." BBVA Mexico, *Documentos de Trabajo* 11, 05 (February).

Andina Migrante. 2012. No. 13, July.

Bhagwati, Jagdish, and William Dellalfar. 1973. "The Brain Drain and Income Taxation." *World Development* 1, 1–2 (February): 94–101.

Bourguignon, Francois. 2007. "Foreword." In Çaglar Özden and Maurice Schiff (eds.), *International Migration, Remittances, and the Brain Drain*. Basingstoke: Palgrave Macmillan.

Canterbury, D. 2012. *Capital Accumulation and Migration*. Leiden: Brill.

____. 2010. "The Development Impact of Migration under Neoliberal Capitalism." *Migración y Desarrollo* 8, 15: 5–42.

Carling, J. 2005. "Gender Dimensions of International Migration." Background Paper. Geneva: GCIM.

Carrington, William, and Enrica Detraglache. 1998. "How Big Is the Brain Drain?" IMF *Working Paper* No. 98/102.

Castles, S., and R. Delgado Wise (eds.). 2008. *Migration and Development: Perspectives from the South*. Geneva: OIM.

Commission on Human Security. 2003. Human Security Now. New York: CHS.

Davies, J.B., S. Sandström, A. Shorroks and E.N. Wolff. 2008. "The World Distribution of Household Wealth." In James B. Davies (ed.), *Personal Wealth from a Global Perspective*. Oxford: Oxford University Press.

De Haas, Hein. 2008. "Migration and Development: A Theoretical Perspective." *Working Paper* 9, International Migration Institute, University of Oxford.

Delgado Wise, Raúl. 2015. "Unraveling Mexican Highly-Skilled Migration in the Context of Neoliberal Globalization." In S, Castles, M. Arias Cubas and D. Ozkul (eds.), *Social Transformation and Migration: National and Local Experiences in South Korea, Turkey, México and Australia*. United Kingdom: Paldgrave MacMillan.

____. 2009. "Dynamics of Forced Migration and the Dialectic of Migration and Development." Critical Sociology 35, 6: 767–84.

Docquier, Frederic, Caglar Ozden and Giovanni Peri. 2011. "The Wage Effects of Immigration and Emigration." *Policy Research Working Paper* 5556. World Bank, Development Research Group, February.

Donato, Katherine, Donna Gabaccia, Jennifer Holdaway, Martin Manalansan and Patricia Pessar. 2006. "A Glass Half Full? Gender in Migration Studies." *International Migration Review* 40: 3–26.

Fajnzylber, Pablo, and Humberto López. 2007. *The Development Impact of Remittances in Latin America*. Washington, DC: The World Bank.

Foster, J.B., R.W. McChesney and J. Jonna. 2011. "The Internationalization of Monopoly Capital." *Monthly Review* 63, 2: 3–18. <http://monthlyreview.org/2011/06/01/the-internationalization-of-monopoly-capital>.

ILO (International Labour Organization). 2003. *Migration Survey 2003: Country Summaries.* Geneva.

Inglehart, Ronald, and Christian Welzel. 2005. *Modernization, Cultural Change and Democracy: The Human Development Sequence.* New York: Cambridge University Press.

Kroll, L. 2013. "Inside the 2013 Billionaires List: Facts and Figures." Forbes, 4 March. <http://www.forbes.com/sites/luisakroll/2013/03/04/inside-the-2013-billionaires list-factsand-figures>.

Kuznetsov, Yevgeny. 2006. *Diaspora Networks and the International Migration Skills: How Countries Can Draw on Their Talent Abroad.* Washington DC: World Bank.

Lozano, Fernando, and Luciana Gandini. 2012. "La migración calificada de México a Estados Unidos: tendencias de la década 2000–2010," *Coyuntura demográfica* 2: 51–55.

Maimbo, Samuel Munzele, and Dilip Ratha. 2005. *Remittances: Development Impact and Future Prospects.* Washington, DC: World Bank.

Nayyar, Deepak. 1994. "International Labor Movements, Trade Flows and Migration Transitions: A Theoretical Perspective." *Asian and Pacific Migration Journal* 3, 1: 7–30.

Nyarko, Yaw. 2011. "The Returns to the Brain Drain and Brain Circulation in Sub-Saharan Africa: Some Computations Using Data from Ghana." NBER Working Paper 16813, February. Cambridge, MA: National Bureau of Economic Research.

Parpart, Jane, and Eudine Barriteau. 2000. *Theoretical Perspectives on Gender and Development.* Ottawa: IDRC.

Petras, James. 2007. "Mesoamerica Comes to North America: The Dialectics of the Migrant Workers' Movement." Retrieved January 6, 2009 from <http://petras.lahaine.org/articulo.php?p=6&more=1&c=1>.

Pieterse, Jan. 2003. *Globalization and Culture.* Rowman & Littlefield.

Piketty, Thomas. 2013. *Capital in the Twenty-First Century.* Cambridge, MA: Belknap Press.

Piper, Nicola. 2005. *Gender and Migration.* Geneva: Global Commission on International Migration (GCIM).

Rowlands, Dana. 2004. "The Effects of Poverty, Environmental Degradation, and Gender Conditions on South-to-North Migration." *Canadian Journal of Development Studies* 25, 4: 555–72.

Taran, P., and E. Geronimi. 2003. "Globalization, Labour and Migration: Protection Is Paramount." Perspectives on Labour Migration 3E. Geneva: ILO.

Terrazas, Aaron. 2011. "Migration and Development: Policy Perspectives from the United States." *MPI Report,* June. Migration Policy Institute.

Tsafack, Virginie Nanhou, and Peter Calkins. 2004. "Rôles de la migration dans la transformation des rapports de genre dans les villages du Mali-Sud." *Canadian Journal of Development Studies* 25, 4: 573–75.

U.N. General Assembly. 2004. Women and International Migration, World Survey on the Role of Women in Development. New York: United Nations.

UNDESA (United Nations Department of Economic and Social Affairs). 2005. *The Inequality Predicament: Report on the World Social Situation.* New York: United Nations.

UNDP (United Nations Development Programme). 2010. *Regional Human Development Report for Latin America and the Caribbean.* New York: United Nations Development Programme.

____. 2009. *Human Development Report 2009: Overcoming Barriers, Human Mobility and Development.* New York: United Nations Development Programme.

United Nations, Division for the Advancement of Women. 2004. "Consultative Meeting on Migration and Mobility and How This Movement Affects Women." Report of the Consultative Meeting Malmö, Sweden 2 to 4 December 2003.

UNRISD (United Nations Research Institute for Social Development). 2005. *Gender Equality: Striving for Justice in an Unequal World.* Geneva: UNRISD.

UNU-IHDP and UNEP. 2012. *Inclusive Wealth Report 2102.* Cambridge: Cambridge University Press.

World Bank. 2013. Migration and Development Brief #20. Washington, DC: WB, Migration and Remittances Unit.

World Commission on the Social Dimension of Globalization. 2004. *A Fair Globalisation — Creating Opportunities for All.* Geneva: ILO.

Chapter 2

Migration Dynamics
of Agrarian Change

Regardless of the diverse and complex issues that have surrounded the idea of development over the past six decades it was undoubtedly advanced as a means of furthering the process of capitalist development — the capitalist development of the forces of production. "Development" can thus be understood in two ways, both as a strategy or project, and as a process. In strategic terms it can be seen as the theoretical representation of an "idea" or "project" — to bring about improvements in the social condition of people in the economically backward areas of the world with a judicious combination of policy, social and institutional changes and international cooperation. In structural terms, development is viewed as a long-term process of social change and institutional reform: to transform a precapitalist, traditional agrarian society into a modern industrial capitalist society and economic system (a process of capitalist development, industrialization and modernization).

Development as Process — Evolution of a System

In structural terms, the development process of long-term change in the evolution of large-scale societies has been conceptualized in terms of three alternative meta-theories, each with its own historical narrative. One of these meta-theories/narratives concerns the transformation of an agriculture-based economy and agrarian society into a modern industrial system via a process of industrialization. It is possible to place countries in the process of this transformation into three categories of evolutionary development: preindustrial, industrializing and industrialized. It is assumed that progress in the human or social condition achieved by a society can be measured in terms of "economic growth," or the rate of annual increases in the country's total output of goods and services (the GDP), and that this progress is commensurate with an evolutionary process of productive transformation, i.e., change in the structure of economic production.

A second meta-theory of long-term social change views the process in terms of a transformation in the values that underpin the institutional structure of the social system. In these terms, the evolution of the system, or the transformation of one system into another, is viewed as a transition from a traditional social system (oriented towards traditional values such as communalism, in which individuals are subordinated to the community of which they are a part at the level of mutual obligation) towards a modern system (in which individuals are free to choose and "achieve" their position rather than have it ascribed to them by "society"). In this evolutionary process societies can be characterized as traditional, modernizing or modern.

The third meta-theory of long-term change, which provides yet another lens through which the process of long-term progressive change can be viewed, is that of capitalist development (the transformation of a pre-capitalist society and economy into a capitalist system). In this conception, the fundamental change in the structure of society is the consequence of a process of social change — the transformation of a society of small-scale agricultural producers ("peasants" in the lexicon of agrarian studies) into a proletariat, a class defined by its status of being dispossessed from any means of production and thereby compelled to exchange its labour-power for a living wage.

These three meta-theories of long-term social change and development — *industrialization, modernization* and *proletarianization* — might well be understood as three different facets or dimensions of the same process — the transformation of a pre-capitalist, traditional and agrarian society into a modern industrial capitalist system, a process which has taken several centuries to unfold and still unfolding in different parts of the global south. In the global north, according to this theory, the process has been virtually completed or was completed sometime in the 1980s if not before, leading to the formation of a post-modern and post-industrial society. In the global south, it is argued, societies for the most part are either underdeveloped or undeveloped, and thus in need of "assistance" in completing the transition towards a modern economy and society.

However, some scholars see the process of productive and social transformation not as a continuum or in linear evolutionary terms, but as discontinuous and dependent on the position of a country within an international division of labour or within the structure of international relations. From this modernization theory perspective, the level of economic development achieved by a country, and its rate of economic growth, depends on the ability of the country to overcome obstacles such as an orientation towards traditional values, the absence or weakness of an appropriate institutional framework, and the lack of individuals with an entrepreneurial bent and access to capital and modern technology. The economists behind the 2008 *World Development Report,* which focuses on the role of agriculture in the economic development process take this view, as do the agrarian economists who have argued (and continue to argue) that modernization and development spells the disappearance or end of the "peasantry," which becomes a passé phenomenon, consigned to the dustbins of history.

The Agrarian Question: Farewell to the Peasantry?

By a number of accounts and diverse theoretical perspectives, the forces of change — primarily industrialization, modernization and proletarianization — that operated on underdeveloped societies in the 1960s and 1970s brought about the partial transformation of a society of small landholding agricultural producers or peasant farmers into a working class. This process was theorized in various ways. Marxist scholars reconstructed capitalist development as an initial process of "primitive accumulation" (the separation of the direct producer from the land and other means of production) followed by a process of "proletarianization" (the conversion of the resulting surplus population into a working class). However, non-Marxist scholars, operating with an alternative theory of capitalist modernization, analyzed the same dynamics using a different discourse but in a not altogether different way, by making reference to a process that would lead to the disappearance of the peasantry as an economic agent and thus as a category of analysis.

In the 1970s this view of structural change, shared by both

Marxist and non-Marxist scholars, gave way to a heated debate between "proletarianists," adherents of Marx's thesis regarding the transformation of the direct agricultural producers into a working class, and the "peasantists," or populists, who argued that the forces of capitalist development and social change were not immutable and that the resilience and resistance of peasants could defuse or derail these forces, allowing for the survival of the peasantry and the sustainability of their rural livelihoods.[1]

After a hiatus of some years — a decade and a half of neoliberal reform — this debate was renewed in a study of the "new rurality" (conditions in rural society in an era of globalization) as well as the dynamic forces of resistance against the neoliberal agenda mounted by the landless workers, indigenous communities and peasant or small producer organizations in the 1990s. Although, by several accounts, this wave of active resistance has abated, the debate continues, with some arguing the inevitability of the disappearance of the peasantry, others arguing very much the contrary.[2]

Development Pathways Out of Rural Poverty

A conception of development as modernization and capitalist development is provided by the economists at the World Bank in its 2008 World Development Report (hereafter WDR-08), which focused on "agriculture for development" and diverse "pathways out of (rural) poverty." The economists at the Bank conceive of development as a protracted but incessant process of structural change that inevitably brings about possible conditions for economic growth. A process of productive and social transformation (modernization and capitalist development but urbanization rather than industrialization) paves the way out of poverty for the rural poor.

In their study on rural poverty in Latin America, De Janvry and Sadoulet (2000) observed four strategies for getting out of poverty: (1) an exit strategy; (2) an agricultural strategy; (3) a pluriactive strategy (a mix of agriculture and wage labour); and (4) a development assistance strategy. They conclude that approaches and programs that are participatory seek to identify the needs of the rural poor in order to better target development programs that assist the poor in their strategy of choice (408). According to the WDR-08, for which De Janvry served as the lead author, there are three fundamental development pathways out of rural poverty, each involving an adjustment to the forces of change operating on the poor: farming, labour and migration.

As for farming, it turns out that it provides an avenue of mobility out of poverty for very few in that it requires peasants to become other than they are — major transformation of the direct small-scale agricultural producer into an entrepreneur or capitalist, preferably both, in order to access credit, markets and technology and to mobilize the available productive resources. The driving force behind this social transformation is capitalist development of agriculture, which entails both a concentration of landholding and a technological conversion of production based on a significant increase in the rate of productive investment (in modernizing or upgrading production technology). The pressures on farming to increase the productivity of agricultural labour via technological upgrading or modernization (increasing the capital intensity of production) are immense.

Agricultural activity under these conditions is clearly not an option for the vast majority of peasants, who are therefore encouraged, if not compelled, to abandon agriculture, and for many also the countryside, in order to migrate in the search for better opportunities for self advancement or more productive economic activity. In this situation there are essentially two pathways out of poverty (excluding resistance). One of them is wage labour — a strategy that large numbers of the rural poor are already pursuing. If the statistics on rural household incomes are any indication, over 50 percent of rural householders acquire over half of their income from non-farming activities, i.e., off-farm wage labour.

The other pathway out of poverty is migration, one that many of the rural poor have opted for by moving either to cities in the country or further abroad. The theory behind this development model, constructed by Arthur Lewis (1954), is that the countryside constitutes a massive reservoir of surplus labour, pushing the rural poor off the farms, and that the greater opportunity for wage-remunerated labour in the cities pulls the displaced rural proletariat into the cities, absorbing them into the labour force of an expanding capitalist nucleus of urban-based industry. However, research into the dynamics of this rural-to-urban migratory process suggests that the outcome of the forces of change and development do not confirm this theory. For one thing, in the 1980s the nucleus of capitalist industry did not expand, thus generating an enormous supply of migrant labour surplus to the absorptive capacity of the urban labour market, leading to the growth instead of a burgeoning informal sector of unregulated and unstructured economic activity. Essentially, rural to urban migrants were not working for wages in industrial plants, factories and offices but instead on their own account in the streets. It has been estimated (Klein and Tokman 2000) that in the 1980s and into the 1990s, at least 80 percent of new employment opportunities in the growing urban economies were generated in the "informal sector," which in many underdeveloped countries in Latin America and Asia by the 1990s constituted around 40 percent of the urban economically active population. As Mike Davis (2006) documented with reference to a Marxist theory of surplus labour, this new urban proletariat is associated with the growth of a "planet of slums" as well as peri-urban areas with a floating surplus population with one foot in the urban economy and the other in the rural communities.

Another manifestation of the presumption that labour and migration constitute the most effective pathways out of rural poverty is a belief that is deeply embedded in modernization theory, which dominated analysis and practice in the 1950s and 1970s and is evidently shared by World Bank economists even today (see the Bank's 2008 *World Development Report*). The belief has the following components:

1. the dominant form of agricultural production, the small-scale agricultural producer or peasant farmer, is economically backward, marginal and unproductive;
2. the peasant economy of small-scale localized production is a drag on development;
3. capital invested in urban-based industry has a considerably greater return, with much greater multiplier effects on production and employment, than a comparable investment in agriculture;

4. development requires, and is predicated on, a modernization process of structural transformation — of agriculture into industry and the peasantry into a working class;

5. rural society and agriculture in this process serve development as a reservoir of labour surplus to the requirements of capitalist development and modernization;

6. farming opportunities for the rural poor, most of whom are engaged in relatively unproductive economic activities and are either landless or near landless, are scarce and restricted because either the limits of land reform have been reached or because of the requirements of capitalist modernization (large or increased-scale production, capital-intensive technology, external inputs, access to markets, etc.);

7. many of the rural poor who retain some access to land are compelled to turn towards wage labour as a source of livelihood and household income; and

8. because of the economic and social structure of agricultural production, there are simply too many people in rural society chasing too few opportunities for productive economic activity. Thus, farming provides few "opportunities" for the rural poor to change and improve their situation — to escape or alleviate their poverty.

The combination of these ideas has led many development economists — including the lead authors of the World Bank's *World Development Report 2008* — to view the peasantry as an anachronism, a futile effort to defend a way of life and an economy that is inherently nonviable, entrenching rural dwellers in a poverty trap. The best, if not the only pathway out of this dilemma, is to abandon farming and migrate in the search of wage-labour employment opportunities and inclusion in government services, also more accessible in the cities and urban centres.

National and International Dynamics of Labour Migration

According to Marx's theory of the general law of capital accumulation, the process of capitalist development and proletarianization hinges on the formation of a floating and stagnant army of surplus labour that is absorbed when, where and as needed for the expansion of capital. By the 1980s this process had fuelled massive migration from the countryside to the urban centres on the periphery of the system. However, within the institutional and policy framework of the new world order, the forces of change that had been operating on regional and local scale, restricted by the social structure of capital accumulation, began to expand and operate globally. It would take several decades of capitalist development under a neoliberal regime before the global dynamics of these forces asserted themselves as an identifiable trend, but by the turn into a new millennium, towards the end of what Harvey (2007) termed a short history of neoliberalism, the outcome was clear: the formation of a global labour force fuelled by diverse regional reservoirs of surplus labour. Although the mobility of this labour, relative to movement of capital, is restricted and regulated by the migration policies of the states at the centre of the global capitalist system, there is little question about migration's role as a lever of global capital accumulation.

The nature and characteristics of this role, however, have been subjected to different interpretations. From the perspective of the economists at the World Bank, a perspective that is widely shared by development scholars, this migration has significant development implications. For one, it provides a means of absorbing the mass of surplus labour generated by the capitalist development of agriculture. It is evident that the urban centres in the country and elsewhere in the region do not have the capacity to absorb much of this surplus labour. Also, migration provides a pathway out of rural poverty and an avenue of social mobility and human development (the expansion of choice and increased opportunities for self-realization) for workers. Further, via the mechanism of remittances, the construction of a cross-border labour force and a network of transnational migrant communities, migrant labour contributes both directly and indirectly to local community-based development in the countryside as well as the accumulation of capital and wealth in the urban centres. Researchers in the College of Development at the China Agricultural University (CAU) have established that up to one-third of the country's peasants are "on the road" (some 230 million in 2009) — mobilized for industrial development as "workers" (Jingzhong et al. 2013: 1119). The contribution of this mass of proletarianized and semi-proletetarianized "peasants" to the country's economic development over the past three decades is difficult to determine precisely, but undoubtedly it has been considerable. Cao (2005) calculates that with an average annual payment of around 8000 yuan, each peasant worker creates a surplus value of 17,000 yuan a year.

But researchers associated with the International Network on Migration and Development provide a very different perspective on this migration process. As Delgado Wise (2009) constructs it, labour migration to the U.S. and Europe in the context of neoliberal globalization allows "capital" in the north of a global development divide to appropriate the human resources and labour power of countries and regions in the global south without having to bear the costs of accumulating these resources and reproducing this vast reservoir of labour power.

Towards a New Paradigm:
The Search for Another Form of Development

In the 1980s development thinking proceeded along two lines within the dominant paradigm. The dominant form of development thinking and analysis might be termed "structuralist" in one form or the other — East European and Latin American in the main. This structuralist approach was manifest in the theory that the economic and social structure of societies in the economically backward areas inhibited "development," which required institutional reform and planned actions by the state. Given the weakness in the institutional development of the market and the lack of a capitalist class prepared to assume responsibility for the "function of capital" — investment, entrepreneurship and enterprise management — it was generally assumed that the state would have to step in and replace the private sector in this regard. On the other side of the debate on development economics could be found proponents of the theory that the problem was not in the economic structure of society as much as the lack of institutional support for the market, which, if left to operate freely would ultimately lead to improvements and change — and a more optimal distribution of society's productive resources. In the

1960s this liberal non-structuralist line was maintained almost alone by Alfred Schultz, a prominent member of the neoliberal thought collective organized by Von Hayek. But by 1980, in the context of what was perceived to be the failures of state-led development, government intervention in the economy and interference with the market (via regulations and protectionism, etc.), the solitary voice of Schultz was joined by many others, giving rise to what Toye (1987) and others view as a conservative counter-revolution in development thinking and practice — and a new world order based on neoliberal globalization.

The turn towards neoliberal globalization — free market capitalism — in the 1980s was but one of several new currents of development thinking within the mainstream. Another current could be termed "social liberalism" (rather than "neoliberalism"). While neoliberalism can be seen as another formulation of the idea of economic progress, the social liberal line of development thinking entailed a fusion of the ideas of equity (equality of opportunity) and freedom (expansion of choice) within an emerging basic needs paradigm (Sen 1999; Haq 1995; Stewart 2008).

Within the institutional and policy framework of the social liberalism paradigm there emerged the search for an alternative form of development, initiated from below and within rather than from above and the outside. By the end of the decade this search for "another development" had assumed the form and scale of a global movement concerned with creating a "new paradigm" in development thinking and practice (Chopra, Kadekodi and Murty 1990; Stewart 2008). Thinking about development within this "new paradigm" took diverse forms but was unified by a general agreement in principle, a fundamental consensus that development should be equitable and socially inclusive, human in scale and form, sustainable in terms of the environment and livelihoods, participatory and empowering of the poor, capacitating them to act for themselves, to be the agents of their own development (Cohen and Uphoff 1977).

With this consensus, and on this conceptual foundation of the ideas of equity and freedom, the search for "another development" was advanced in several directions, and several models were constructed. The most consequential model, as it turned out, was constructed by the economists[3] associated with the United Nations Development Programme (UNDP), which in 1990 initiated an annual publication of its *Human Development Report* dedicated to the monitoring of the progress made by different countries in the direction of "human development," a development regime that "put(s) people at the centre of development," designed so as to allow people to "realize their potential, increase their choices and enjoy ... the freedom to lead lives they value" (UNDP 2009).

As with the *World Development Report* 2008, the HDR-09 focuses on migration as a major pathway out of rural poverty. As with the WDR-08, the HDR-09 identifies education as the major avenue of social mobility and mechanism for development, for the expansion of choices available to individuals and capacitating them to take advantage of their opportunities.

Migration, both within and beyond national borders, an increasingly prominent theme in domestic and international debates, is the topic of the HDR-09. The starting point of this report is that the global distribution of capabilities is extraordinarily unequal and that this is a major driver for the movement of people, a major incentive to migrate. Migration can expand an individual's choices — in terms of incomes, accessing services and participation, for example. But the opportunities open to people vary from those who are best endowed to those with limited skills and assets. These underlying inequalities are rooted in the institutional structure of society but can be compounded by policy distortions. This is a major theme of the report. The HDR-09 investigates the migration process in the context of demographic changes and trends in both economic growth and social inequality. It also presents more detailed and nuanced analysis of individual, family and village experiences and explores the less visible movements typically pursued by disadvantaged groups, such as short-term and seasonal migration.

In the HDR-09, the UNDP reviews a range of evidence about the positive impacts of migration on human development through such avenues as increased household incomes and improved access to education and health services. The authors of the report present evidence that migration can empower traditionally disadvantaged groups, in particular women. At the same time, the report cautions, there are risks to human development where and when migration is a reaction to threats and the denial of choice, and where regular opportunities for movement are constrained.

In the context of these constraints, the report argues, national and local policies can play a critical role in enabling better human development outcomes for both those who choose to move in order to improve their circumstances, and those forced to relocate due to conflict, environmental degradation and the like. For one thing, host country restrictions can raise both the costs and the risks of migration. Similarly, negative outcomes can arise at the country level where basic civic rights, such as voting, schooling and health care, are denied to those who have moved across provincial lines to work and live. The HDR-09 shows how a human development approach can be a means to redress some of the underlying issues that erode the benefits of mobility and forced migration.

Conclusion

The capitalist development of the forces of production has brought about a process of social change, transforming an agrarian society based on a traditional communal culture of social solidarity into a modern industrial system formed around the capital-labour relation, the exchange of labour power for a living wage or salary. A critical feature of this process is the transformation of direct small-holding peasant farmers into a working class — a proletariat of wage labourers and an industrial reserve army of surplus rural labour. The productive and social transformations associated with the capitalist development process have been, and continue to be, fuelled by the migration of peasant farmers, separated in different ways from their means of production and forced to abandon agriculture and their traditional way of life and livelihood. Development theorists in the tradition of modernization theory expressed this dynamic in terms of the notion of the existence in the agricultural sector of an "unlimited supply of surplus labour" that could be mobilized and harnessed in the interest of economic development. The aim and purpose of "development," the shared objective of the organizations and individuals engaged in the project of international cooperation, is to alleviate poverty and assist the "rural poor" in taking one of the development pathways out of rural poverty (agriculture, labour and migration) and to capacitate the poor for entry into the labour market.

Notes

1. On this debate — Marxism and economic populism — see Otero (1999) as well as Bernstein (2012) and Van der Ploeg (2015), who represent polar positions.
2. On this debate, see two earlier publications in the ICAS series — Bernstein (2012) and Van der Ploeg (2015).
3. Including and in particular Fukuda-Parr, Sakiko, Kumar, Griffin, Knight, Sen, Haq and Stewart.

References

Bernstein, Henry. 2012. *Class Dynamics of Agrarian Change*. Halifax: Fernwood Publishing.

Cao, L. 2005. "How Much Have Peasant Workers Contributed to China?" Xiao Xiang Morning News. <http://finance.stockstar.com/SS2005090230262226.shtml>.

Chopra, K., G. Kadekodi and M. Murty. 1990. *Participatory Development*. London: Sage.

Cohen, J.M., and N.T. Uphoff. 1977. *Rural Development Participation: Concepts and Measure for Project Design, Implementation and Evaluation*. Ithaca NY: Cornell University, Centre for International Studies.

Davis, Mike. 2006. *A Planet of Slums*. London: Verso.

De Janvry, Alain, and Elisabeth Sadoulet. 2000. "Rural Poverty in Latin America: Determinants and Exit Paths." *Food Policy* 25: 389–409.

Delgado Wise, Raúl. 2009. "Dynamics of Forced Migration and the Dialectic of Migration and Development." Critical Sociology 35, 6: 767–84.

Haq, Mahbub Ul. 1995. *Reflections on Human Development*. New York: Oxford University Press.

Harvey, David. 2007. *A Brief History of Neoliberalism*. Oxford University Press.

Jingzhong, Ye, Chunyu Wang, Huifang Wu, Congzhi He and Juan Liu. 2013. "Internal Migration and Left-Behind Populations in China." *Journal of Peasant Studies* 40, 6: 1119–46.

Klein, E., and V. Tokman. 2000. "La estratificación social bajo tension en la era de la globalización." *Revista de CEPAL* 72 (Deciembre): 7–30.

Lewis, W. Arthur. 1954. "Economic Development with Unlimited Supplies of Labor." *Manchester School of Economic and Social Studies* 22: 139–91.

Otero, Gerardo. 1999. *Farewell to the Peasantry? Political Class Formation in Rural Mexico*. Boulder, CO: Westview.

Sen, Amartya. 1999. *Development As Freedom.* NY: Alfred A. Knopf.

Stewart, Francis. 2008. "Human Development as an Alternative Development Paradigm." UNDP. <http://hdr.undp.org/en/media/1>.

Toye, John. 1987. *Dilemmas of Development: Reflections on the Counter-Revolution in Development Theory and Policy.* Oxford: Basil Blackwell.

UNDP (United Nations Development Programme). 2009. *Human Development Report 2009: Overcoming Barriers, Human Mobility and Development.* New York: United Nations Development Programme.

Van der Ploeg, Jan. 2015. Peasants and the Art of Agriculture: A Chayanov Manifesto. Halifax: Fernwood Publishing.

World Bank. 2008. *World Development Report 2008. Agriculture for Development.* Washington, DC: World Bank.

Chapter 3

Global Capital, Migrant Labour and the Nation-State

There are three principal themes of this chapter. First, as was noted by Robin Cohen in *The New Helots* (1987), many migrant workers are still locked into forms of labour exploitation that marked the birth of global capitalism. Second, also emphasized by Cohen, employer demand for cheap and often illegal forms of labour has not abated despite the spread of a fundamentalist and utopian belief in capitalism with unregulated market forces — that under free market capitalism economic opportunities for self-advancement are available to everyone. Whether manufacturing is exported to low-wage areas or migrants are imported to work in metropolitan service sectors, the distinctions between established workers, privileged foreigners and helot labourers have remained and by some accounts have even deepened (see Cohen, Chapter 6). Third, politicians in migrant-importing states have been zealous in policing their frontiers in the name of "national security" as a strategy not only to prevent economic migrants from flooding the labour market and legal migrants from "masquerading" as political refugees in order to take advantage of social welfare programs and free public education, but mainly to "justify" the permanent violation of migrants' human and labour rights, diminish labour costs and impose corporate-driven migration policies. This strategy has been labelled in the literature as "migration management" (Delgado Wise, Márquez and Puentes 2013). In the case of the United States, the destination point of millions of migrants from Mexico, Central and South America, the migration management approach has been quite successful increasing profits and fiscal gains for both employers and the host local and federal governments. Moreover, as Geiger and Pécoud argue, "Many measures to stop unauthorized migration or to prevent refugees to claim asylum are, for example, presented as 'necessary' to fight human smuggling and trafficking.… This victimhood approach seems to have replaced any kind of binding commitments to safeguard migrants' rights" (Geiger and Pécoud 2010: 13).

The Capitalist Labour Market:
From Unfree Slave Labour to Free Wage Labour

Capitalism in theory is based on "free labour" — the free exchange by workers of their labour power for a living wage. But can a wage labourer be described as free? As Cohen (2006: 13) notes, the very concept of "labour" implies at least some degree of compulsion. Citing Womack, he points out that for about 2,500 years western cultures distinguished between "labour" and "work." In every European language, Womack writes, "labour meant pain, effort, pangs, penalty, strain, drudgery, struggle, battle, suffering, grief, distress, poverty, loneliness, abandonment, ordeal, adversity, trouble. Work meant making, building, providing, causing, accomplishment, completion, satisfaction" (13).

To understand the notion of free labour — a "free" labourer under capitalism — we need to start with Marx's central idea, which we expounded in Chapter 2, that the working class is formed in a process of "primitive accumulation," which entails the separation of the direct small landholding agricultural producer or peasant farmer from the land and thus their basic means of social production. In this process of "primitive" accumulation, "great masses of men are suddenly and forcibly torn from their means of subsistence, and hurled onto the labour-market as free, unprotected and rightless proletarians" (Marx 1954: 876).

For Marx, the social transformation of peasant farmers into wage labourers comprises two elements. First, workers are no longer simply a means of production, as was the case with a slave or serf. They are therefore free of any direct proprietorial rights exercised over them. Second, dispossessed from their own means of production and subsistence (land, tools) and denied access to customary use of the commons, they are free in a sense, but perforce compelled to exchange their one remaining possession, their labour, in exchange for a living wage.

Free labour so understood was the result of a complicated historical process, which can be traced back to the origins and evolution of capitalism. In the sixteenth century, we had what some theorists describe as the origins of the "world capitalist system," although strictly speaking the system was not capitalist in the sense that mercantile capital did not rely on free wage labour.[1] Rather it relied on semi-feudal relations of agricultural production (serfdom) on the *latifundia* and slave labour in the mines and on the plantations. Millions of enslaved Africans were imported to work on the sugar plantations of the West Indies and in Brazil. Wages were paid to workers in the mines but under conditions that can best be described as slave labour, and these miners were oppressed and by no means free to contract their labour. Capital was indeed accumulated in this "world system of colonial oppression," as Lenin understood it in his study of *Imperialism, the Highest Stage of Capitalism*, but not on the basis of free wage labour[2]; rather it was by means of enslavement and unfree wage labour in the extraction of gold and silver, state-sanctioned piracy and "commerce," and financial strangulation of the overwhelming majority of the population of the world by a handful of advanced countries.

Regarding international labour migration there are several important considerations. First, just as capital tends to move from one place to another, and from one country to another, in search of profit, so does labour, overcoming many obstacles and in many cases at a major personal cost, move in order to make a living and escape destitution and unemployment in places where capitalism has failed to develop altogether, or is insufficiently developed, or is in decline, to the centres of its expansion, given a propensity towards uneven development. That is, capitalism constitutes a strong "pull factor" for people with few or no alternatives. Second, in many if not all cases the impulse or decision to migrate is "forced" in the sense that the migrants are often dispossessed and pushed off the land and thus separated from any means of obtaining a livelihood. And, needless to say, slave labour is entirely forced. Indeed, the export and import of labour in the form of the slave trade is better understood as commerce in a tradeable commodity (slave labour) than migration, which implies a measure of decision-making and choice. The birth of capitalism in the mid-1850s, in the form of wage labour — the formation of a working class — and the factory system, marked the slow death knell of slavery, even on the plantation economies where it was gradually replaced with indentured labour.

Slave Labour and Mercantile Capitalism

Systemic large-scale migration is unique to capitalism. The dynamics of capitalist development obliges workers, through physical or economic compulsion, to move from one part of a country to another, or from one country or continent to another, thus necessitating both internal and international migration. In capitalism's earliest days, this movement took the form of the slave trade — the first forced, large-scale migration movement of labour in history. Thirty million Africans were enslaved and transported across the Atlantic to the New World; only 11 million survived the journey. Jamaica and the rest of the British West Indies were turned into colonial labour camps in "a traffic so beneficial to the nation," in the words of a British secretary of state in 1774.

Slave labour and the slave trade were crucial factors in the evolution of capitalism — in the generation of great fortunes that were invested in the new production technologies of the Industrial Revolution and the supply of labour-power, made available in Great Britain by means of enclosing the commons in the countryside.[3] Great Britain's role in the transport of African slaves on such a vast scale in the sixteenth and seventeenth centuries gave it a head start and helped to kick start the Industrial Revolution. Apart from reflecting on the inhumanity of the British ruling class, the transport of 30 million enslaved people across the Atlantic satisfied the colossal demand for labour that marked the dawn of capitalism. The slave trade and the use of slave labour in the plantation economy of the British Caribbean were also critical factors in the evolution of capitalism in Europe and the United States, and in what has been described as the "development of underdevelopment" on the periphery of the capitalist world economy — the underdevelopment of Africa, the Caribbean and Latin America (Blackburn 1998; Rodney 1972; Williams 1944). As Marx argued, "the veiled slavery of the wage-workers in Europe needed, for its pedestal, slavery pure and simple in the new world" (1954: 711).

The ruling capitalist class in Europe used their control of international trade to ensure that Africa specialized in exporting captive people for their labour and that Latin America was a major source of bullion and commercial profit. Right through the 1600s and 1700s, and for much of the 1800s, Europeans continued to make extraordinary profits from the extraction of natural resources and the super-exploitation of enslaved labour in the plantations and indigenous labour in the gold and silver mines of the New World (Blackburn 1998). These profits continued to be re-invested in Western Europe into such areas as shipping, insurance, the formation of companies, capitalist agriculture, technology and the manufacture of machinery.

Trading in enslaved Africans, according to Cohen (2006), was not only a major factor in the evolution of capitalism in Europe but it speeded up Europe's technological development. For example, he notes that the evolution of European shipbuilding from the 1500s to the 1800s was a logical consequence of their monopoly of sea commerce in that period. Technological developments (and the technological conversion of capitalist production), as Blackburn (1998) established, were funded with transatlantic slave trade money. For example, James Watts reportedly expressed eternal gratitude to the West Indian slave owners who directly financed his famous steam engine (Cohen 2006). Their money allowed him to take his designs from the drawing board to the factory.

Indentured Labour in the Transition to Industrial Capitalism

Social institutions as powerful as slavery do not collapse overnight. Slavery was abolished in British colonies in 1834, but only children under the age of six were immediately freed; the remaining former slaves were "apprenticed" to their masters for four to six years. Slavery survived until 1863 in the Dutch colonies and 1865 in the United States (Cohen 2006: Chapter 1). Vagrancy laws, apprenticeship, contracts and economic compulsion continued to tie many former slaves to their old tasks. However, as a profitable and preferred means of organizing labour the system was clearly on its way out. Moreover, the plantation owners of the time, who were addicted to and the major users of slave labour, knew it. As Adam Smith argued in *The Wealth of Nations*, "the work done by slaves although it appears to cost only their maintenance is in the end the dearest of any" (cited in Tinker 1974: 77). The planters had to maintain a year-round labour force in a seasonal industry while the slaves had to be supervised, policed, housed, clothed and fed. Similarly, British humanitarians maintained that "free labour" would be more efficient than slave labour. The planters agreed. One, in Mauritius, in an account provided by Cohen (2006: 40), "rubbed his hands in glee at the arrival of the first group of Indian indentured labourers in 1835. 'Their cost,' he gloated, 'is not half that of a slave.'" The system of indentureship thus rapidly replaced slavery as the key mechanism of exploitation in the European plantation economies.

The indenture system, which was also used to finance the flow of European migrant labour to North America, did not mean free labour. Indentured workers were "free" only insofar as they could not be owned, bought or sold. The workers were highly constrained until the expiry of the indenture contract, the breach of which was met by prosecution and often by severe punishment (Northrup 1995).

Indenture was a common form of international labour recruitment from 1835, when slavery was being phased out, to 1941, when, according to Potts (1990: 63–103), it met its demise with the revocation of the Coolie Ordinance in the Dutch colonies. Potts (1990: 72–73) estimates that, over this period, anywhere between 12 and 37 million workers were recruited under this arrangement, mostly to supply labour to the British colonies and other European colonial possessions. According to Cohen, in British India, a principal source of supply of indentured labour, the system effectively came to an end in 1920, partly as the result of Indian nationalist objections, but also because the labour supply to the plantation economies by then was sufficient to meet the demand.

The plantation economies established in the Caribbean and Brazil within the institutional and policy framework of mercantile capitalism predominantly deployed slave, indentured and contract labourers from Africa and Asia. However, it is important to remember Williams's (1944: 7) corrective that "unfree labour in the New World was brown, white, black and yellow; Catholic, Protestant and pagan." He showed that before the planters turned to Africa, "redemptioners," convicts and white servants from Ireland, Britain, Portugal, Madeira and elsewhere, were sent to the West Indies, where small communities descended from these groups still survive today.

However, most European migrants did not go to the plantation colonies but to the United States of America and to what are sometimes described as "colonies of settlement" (New Zealand, Canada, Australia, Rhodesia and South Africa in the British case; Brazil, Mozambique and Angola in the Portuguese case; Indonesia for the Dutch; and Algeria and Tunisia in the case of the French).[4] Many of these migrants, anxious to escape the harsh conditions and super-exploitation of "free" wage labour in the factories that sprang up in the heartlands of British and European industrial capitalism, travelled to the agricultural frontier in the "new world" in search of land to work on their own account rather than for wages, so much so that budding capitalists and farm owners in Canada, for example, despaired of finding a labour force for their farms and factories. Nevertheless, many European immigrants were too poor to acquire land or toil for themselves, or were indentured until they were able to pay back the costs of their travel and avail themselves of the "free" wage labour opportunities provided by the labour market under capitalism.

The last two decades of the nineteenth century and the first two of the twentieth saw one of the largest demographic shifts in recorded history, based on a massive flow of migrant workers. The largest stream in this flow of migrant labour was from Europe to the U.S. and Canada, fuelling the capitalist development of the forces of production in both industry and agriculture, and in the process generating enormous reserves of surplus agricultural labour that were slowly but surely absorbed by the labour markets in the "expanding capitalist nuclei" of the rapidly growing urban centres.

By the end of the Second World War, capitalist development had replaced colonial systems of labour exploitation in the "new world" and many other parts of the world, resulting in the formation of a large proletariat of rural landless workers, which in turn spawned a powerful land struggle and a development process of rural outmigration, urbanization, modernization and industrialization. Although the architects of this development process pushed for rural development and agrarian reform in order to slow down this outmigration, they also encouraged governments to help capacitate rural migrants for entry into the urban labour market — to provide a source of cheap labour for capitalist industry.

The new world order of capitalist development, brought about in the 1980s under the aegis of the Washington consensus on the virtues of free market capitalism, facilitated the penetration of capital and the transition towards capitalism in the agricultural sector of economies and societies in Latin America and elsewhere on the periphery of the world capitalist system. However, it also led to the destruction of forces of production in both agriculture and industry, which both fuelled and accelerated a process of rural-to-urban migration.

Given the relative lack of productive investment in industry, and in the 1990s the influx of capital in the form of private foreign direct investment, the involution of urban labour markets and the consequent absence of the economic opportunities held out by the development community to the masses of rural landless workers flocking to the cities opened up international migration as a new development pathway out of rural poverty. The World Bank in its flagship annual publication, *The Development Report* — particularly in its 2008 report on the role of agriculture for development — always flagged labour and migration as major development pathways out of rural poverty. The role of governments in the development strategy laid out in these reports was both to facilitate the capitalist development (or modernization) of agriculture and to capacitate recent rural migrants for entry into the labour market. However, by the mid-1990s it was evident that the theorized economic opportunities of the labour market had not materialized, leading the economists at the Bank, together with those at ECLAC, to design a new development model and formulate a strategy that would lead in theory to both inclusive development and the empowerment of the poor. Key elements of this two-pronged sociocentric strategy[5] were to assist the rural poor to stay in their rural communities by diversifying their sources of household income, including, on part of governments a program of conditional cash transfers, and on part of the rural poor to use remittances both for income support and for productive investment in the community. There is now a robust academic and policy debate on this issue, but on the World Bank's position, see in particular Mendes Pereira (2014).

Migration and the Capitalist Labour Market

Migrants are generally motivated to leave their homeland and their community in search of a better life and more economic opportunities overseas or abroad. Migration economists write of diverse "push" and "pull" factors, with reference to both the objective and subjective conditions behind the decisions of individuals and families to migrate. However, the dominant stream of migrant individuals and families are in the search of better employment and work opportunities — they seek improved and more secure livelihoods and income by selling their labour-power on the labour market. In other words, they are migrant workers.

The international and global flow of migrant workers today is voluminous, notwithstanding the restrictions put into place by the governments of recipient countries. It is estimated that annual global flow of migrants — people and families on the move for diverse reasons but primarily because of poverty, displacement or persecution — is in the order of millions (migrant inflows in Europe and the U.S. together exceeding five million a year) and that, according to the Global Commission on International Migration (GCIM) in 2006, migrant workers constitute at least two-thirds of this flow.[6] The other third is composed of families and individuals who choose or are pushed to migrate because of environmental or political reasons, i.e., they are refugees seeking to escape the consequences of a natural disaster or changing environment conditions or political conditions (persecution, war, etc.) in their country of origin.

For migrant workers, the most critical issue regarding where to migrate is the labour market in the chosen or recipient country, i.e., the degree to which the type of labour they can offer is in demand. As a point of fact, researchers have discovered, and migrants know all too well, that governments in the recipient countries actively discriminate against forms of labour that are not in demand and actively promote the flow of migrant labour in high demand. However, the state of the labour market is by no means the only structural factor behind the decision as to where to migrate; the existing pattern of migrant labour flow suggests that other factors than the market are at work. For one thing, migrants are often not knowledgeable of the market. For another, migration patterns show a strong connection with what might be termed economic imperialism and colonialism. Thus, South and Central Americans and Mexicans predominantly migrate north to the U.S., and to a much lesser extent Canada. Of course, the U.S. historically has been the dominant economic power in Latin America. Migrants from North Africa and Sub-Saharan Africa migrate predominantly north to Europe, usually to countries that were most active in their colonial past. Of course, contiguity or closeness, and thus accessibility and cost, are also factors at play here. And another factor seems to be prior migration patterns. Thus, migrants tend to track prior movements via family and community members and choose to migrate to areas where there has formed a sizeable community of migrants from their country. Thus, migrants from Zacatecas, the Mexican state with the largest outflow of migrant workers as a percentage of state population, predominantly migrate to Chicago and Los Angeles, where there exist substantial communities and migrant clubs formed by earlier generations of migrant workers from Zacatecas (Cypher and Delgado-Wise 2007). In fact, direct daily flights to these cities have been set up to handle the constant trans-border flow within migrant families of Zacatecan origin.

Studies of migrant labour flows vis-à-vis the labour market do not show a consistent patterns as to the type of labour that is attracted or even fast tracked. The determining factor appears to be labour demand and the adjustment or response of government policy to changes in demand — not in terms of "labour matching" but to assure a permanent supply of cheap and flexible labour, including an irregular or undocumented workforce. Thus, the agricultural sector in the southern states of the U.S. has drawn on an inexhaustible supply of *espaldas mojadas* as day labourers to harvest fruits and vegetables, very badly paid and backbreaking work for which there is an inadequate domestic supply and a ready supply just across the border. Both demand and supply — or "push" and "pull" — factors seem to be creating one of the largest flows of seasonal and permanent migrant labour in the world — both officially sanctioned and "illegal," irregular or undocumented. The same pattern and conditions are found in northern Europe, regarding southern European labour and more recently workers from eastern Europe as well as the near east — Turkey, Iran, etc. — as well as the African continent. Again there are family intergenerational patterns and colonial ties at work — Turkish migrants, for example, preferring Germany and North Africans going to Italy and Spain now that these parts of Europe have advanced in their level of economic growth and development.

However, the condition of the labour market — the demand for specific forms of labour — is clearly a defining if not determining factor, at least as regards regulation of entry, i.e., in response to demand and reduction of labour costs. Thus, the past two decades have witnessed a decided shift from a demand for agricultural and construction industry labour, as well as hotel/restaurant/hospitality workers, towards highly educated labour related to the growing demand in the north for software services and other qualified and trained intellectual labour. In fact, the demand for this type of labour has grown exponentially, so much so that the United Nations Development Programme in 2001 identified a significant new development problem: a brain drain constituted by the loss in the global south not only of their most productive members — a longstanding problem — but the most highly trained and educated individuals, on whom considerable scarce financial resources have been spent. This investment by the migrant-sending countries is "appropriated" for free by the migrant-recipient countries in the north, which have long been the major recipient of this type of highly qualified labour (professionals, scientists, technicians and entrepreneurs). The U.S. and other rich nations have been opening their doors more and more in recent years to professionals from underdeveloped countries, which bear the cost of the production and education of this highly skilled labour force and then loses access to this productive human resource for national development.

This pattern of a south to north brain drain is a growing problem for many underdeveloped countries. For example, the UNDP documented the migration in 2000 from India to the U.S. of 100,000 computer industry workers, a number that is expected to go up as the U.S. government ratchets up the number of visas to highly educated professionals. The UNDP calculates that this drain of university-educated workers costs India US$15,000–20,000 per professional, i.e., as much as $2 billion a year, and this is just in one industry. The overall cost to the underdeveloped countries in the south of this type of emigration is staggering and is enough to seriously undercut the prospect for economic development at home.

This problem is also evident in the shift that has occurred in the pattern and internal structure of Mexican migrant labour. A growing segment of these migrants are university educated and highly trained. In fact, Mexican migrants today on average are better educated than the U.S.'s average, a "productive resource" that is almost entirely lost to Mexico. And indications are that the economic benefits deriving from the most highly qualified, educated and trained streams of labour accrue almost entirely to the migrant recipient countries, such as the U.S., which did not bear any of the not insignificant costs of reproducing this labour.

Further evidence of the brain drain problem comes from the initiatives and concerted efforts of diverse U.N. agencies, development NGOs and technology firms in 2002 to reverse the devastating loss of university educated professionals in Africa. Among those targeted in this initiative are scientists, medical doctors, engineers, university lecturers, economists, information technologists and other highly skilled people in short supply on the continent.

The *Maquiladores,* Migrant Labour and the U.S.–Mexico Border

The U.S. has the highest levels of immigration in the world, absorbing up to 20 percent of all documented global migrants. And Mexico is the U.S.'s biggest source of migrant labour, representing 27 percent of the global flow of such migrants in 2004, and 28 percent ten years later in 2014, according to data from the U.S. Current Population Survey. In addition, it is estimated that the flow of undocumented or irregular migrant workers from Mexico to the U.S. equals the legal flow of such labour. These irregular or undocumented migrant workers add up to six million or so Mexican migrants working "illegally" in the U.S., resulting in a major political debate in the U.S., with Republicans steadfastly refusing to allow the "illegal" migrants to stay and thus jump to the head of the long queue of workers seeking legal entry to the country. In December 2014, the Obama administration used an executive decree to temporarily legalize the status of up to five million of these illegal migrants. It's hard to predict the final outcome of these political maneuverings between the Republicans and Democrats. (The Republicans have promised to reverse these measures, but have to take into account the wrath of Hispanoamericans and potential negative electoral outfall.)

Among the reasons for such huge flows of migrant workers from Mexico to the U.S. is the sorry state of the Mexican economy, which can be traced back in part to the operations of U.S. capital and the multinational corporations that dominate the world economy and in part to NAFTA, the free trade agreement struck between Mexico, Canada and the U.S., in force since January 1994. John Saxe-Fernandez and Omar Núñez (2001), two well-known Mexican political economists, found that U.S. corporations and banks over the course of the 1990s, a decade that saw a large influx of capital in the form of foreign direct investment (FDI) into Latin America, pillaged Mexico of its natural and financial resources, transferring up to \$100 million in the form of profits, bank interest payments and dividends to U.S. investors. One side-effect of this process, associated in Mexico with the implementation of structural adjustment programs[7] and NAFTA, which has subjected hundreds of thousands of poor indigenous and other small and medium-sized producers to the competitive pressures of the "world market" (U.S. state subsidized exports), has been a production crisis of enormous proportions, forcing untold numbers of Mexicans to abandon their communities and to migrate to the U.S. in search of paid work. This could be seen as a supply-side explanation for the export of Mexican labour. On the other side is the labour market in the U.S., driven by labour deficits and a voracious appetite for cheap labour. In this context, it is estimated that entire industries in the U.S., as well as several economies in the south, would collapse were it not for the supply of Mexican documented and undocumented migrant workers, which, until recently, had been concentrated in three sectors: agricultural work, mostly seasonal; services, both in food and beverages/hospitality and related industries and in the sub-sector of personal service, such as maid service, gardening, etc.; and the industrial sector, primarily construction activities. This pattern in the export of Mexican labour, which can also be found in other regions of the world economy, was to some extent counterbalanced in the 1980s by the export of U.S. capital in the form of productive investment in the construction of manufacturing plants employing U.S. capital and Mexican labour: the *maquiladora* system.

According to Cypher and Delgado-Wise (2011), a major impulse behind the *maquiladora* system is to provide an alternative to the importation of cheap Mexican migrant labour. In theory this process is facilitated by NAFTA, a system of multilateral free trade among Mexico, the U.S. and Canada. But in practice NAFTA has worked to expand international trade (creating a free trade zone) and free the movement of U.S. capital from the controls placed on it by the Mexican and Canadian governments. NAFTA has also strengthened the movement by U.S. manufacturing firms to relocate assembly operations to take advantage of cheap labour at source. To import manufacturing workers would entail payment of wages up to five times higher. At the global level this has resulted in a "new international division of labour" and the creation of a globally integrated manufacturing production system. In Mexico, it has also resulted in the construction close to the border of an extensive *maquiladora* system, which employs U.S. capital and technology and Mexican labour, creating a manufacturing export platform and a free enterprise zone with relaxed labour and environmental conditions for the operations of U.S. capital.

In Mexico this has meant an enormous expansion of manufacturing exports, now the biggest source by far of export revenues, leading oil and migrant remittances, the next biggest sources of export earnings. Between 1991 and 2000, exports grew at an annual average rate of 16.3 percent, forming the leading sector of the economy. *Maquiladora* exports were the most dynamic of all, growing at an annual average rate of 19.6 percent. Manufacturing exports rose from less than 25 percent of total exports in 1982 to 84 percent in 2014. Today Mexico is Latin America's top exporter and ranks fifteenth in the hierarchy of exporting countries (Statista 2014). And by 2014 the 6,000 or so *maquiladora* firms that were clustered predominantly along the U.S.–Mexico border employed over two million workers, who generated 55 percent of Mexico's manufactured exports.

Maquiladora firms are also present, to a much lesser degree, in many of the interior Mexican states; 60 percent of such employment is concentrated in the border region (INEGI 2014).

The State and Migration: Holding Migrant Workers at Bay

Contrary to much rhetoric about globalization and the weakening of the state in the face of the hegemonic power of monopoly capital, nation-states continue to play a central and active role in managing outward and inward flows of labour across their boundaries. Back in the nineteenth century, the export of Europe's rural and urban working poor was facilitated by governments that lifted restrictions on emigration, while state bodies, trade unions, and philanthropic and colonization societies made financial assistance available (Hardy 2009, citing Held, McGrew, Goldblatt and Perraton 1999).

The rise of the capitalist state, whose formation was coterminous with the rise of capitalism, saw the establishment of borders and categories of citizenship that demarcated immigrants as a separate group. Before the nineteenth century, it was towns and guilds, not national governments, which determined whether foreigners could work (Strikwerda and Guerin-Gonzales 1993). By the First World War the nation-states at the centre of the world capitalist system had assumed responsibility for controlling or managing the inflow of migrants. Passports were the documentary expression of this and were accompanied by a huge expansion of the immigration bureaucracy to police the system.

By the 1920s, Hardy (2009) notes, most governments had taken steps to control the movement of people. In this connection she quotes Gubbay as follows: "Between them, the states ... carve the populations of the world, each person in principle being the subject of a single state, possessing the privilege of citizenship and the right to freedom of movement within its territory, in particular in order to sell ... labour power within the corresponding labour market" (in Strikwerda and Guerin-Gonzales 1993).

By the end of the Second World War both the capacity and the interest of governments in the political system of world capitalism to control immigration and regulate the labour market had greatly increased. However, tensions among different capitalists with different labour market needs created difficulties for these states as they attempted to manage migration flows, particularly as regards the labour market. This is well illustrated by the heated and ongoing political debates over Mexican migration to the United States. As of July 2007, 1,404 pieces of legislation related to immigration had been introduced by 50 states (Hardy 2009). There were 170 pieces of legislation in 2007 alone, tightening up on illegal migrants and enforced by 11,000 border guards with sophisticated surveillance equipment. This body of laws, designed or related to efforts to regulate the massive inflow of migrants from Central America and Mexico through the U.S.–Mexico border, has grown exponentially since 2007. It is estimated that in this period several hundred thousand Mexicans were admitted legally into the U.S., partly in response to demands of employers in the border states and across the country for access to agricultural labour and to supply the voracious appetite of private firms in the service sector for cheap labour — workers willing to work for wages at or below minimum wage rates.

It is also estimated that the inflow of irregular or undocumented Mexican migrant workers over this period has surpassed the stream of legal migrant workers in the total flow since early 1990. But Mexican immigrant workers are central to U.S. capitalism. The number of migrant Mexican workers in the U.S. has more than doubled since 1995, growing from 2.9 million to 5.9 million in 2012, with a peak of 6.9 million in 2007, the year prior to the eruption of the U.S. economic crisis (Passel and Cohn 2014). In 1995, immigrant workers were concentrated in California and Texas, but nowadays they are much more widely dispersed throughout the whole of the U.S. (American Immigration Law Foundation 2002).

In the immigration literature the requirements of the labour market is but one of a multitude of issues related to the efforts of the government to control the flow of immigrants and migrant workers. However, state measures to "manage" migration have been of enormous ideological and political importance, but they are rarely successful in actually stopping migration when wider social, environmental and economic forces continue to fuel the movement of peoples (see, for example, Alden 2012 and Hanson 2007).

Conclusion

Both the new world order and the neoliberal economic model are predicated on an ideology of free market capitalism, leading to a policy stance of liberating the "forces of economic freedom" (the market, the private sector, multinational forms of capitalist enterprise) and the free movement of both capital and commerce.[8] However, when it comes to labour, another major factor and force of global production, the dominant policy stance is one of control and management of the flow of labour in the global economy. And it is the nation-state that has assumed the role of policing and managing the cross-border flow of migrant labour, with reference not to any economic doctrine but the national interest, particularly as regards the domestic labour market.

The dynamics of immigration policy are very complex, contingent on diverse political and economic considerations and priorities. But notwithstanding increased pressures on many governments at the centre of the world system, especially in Europe, to impose tighter controls on immigration from the global south, increasing numbers of workers are on the move, motivated in many cases by the expectation of greater economic opportunities provided by the labour markets in these countries. Policymakers and politicians are generally divided on the pros and cons of this immigration but in many cases are fully cognizant of the economic advantages they bring to the economy, sufficiently so as to overcome the fear in some sectors and in some countries that these migrants will take away jobs from nationals, not adjust to their culture and way of life, and bring unwanted conflict. For one thing, they are at least dimly — in some cases acutely — aware that that increased immigration often means expansion rather than saturation of labour markets, with increases in jobs and incomes. Both unskilled and highly skilled immigrant workers make a significant contribution to the economies of the recipient societies, as well as their societies and communities back home — or at least this is the view overall of officials in the international development community, including the World Bank and a number of operational agencies of the United Nations system. These officials, in their policy advice to governments engaged in the project of international cooperation, point towards many studies that show that migrant workers, including unskilled immigrant workers, play a vital role in improving standards of living in the developed world by means of their remitted earnings. These remittances, these reports show, now constitute a major source of household income in many rural communities and revenues with which to balance the country's national accounts. Reports provided by the international organizations that participate in the project of international cooperation also support the view of those who argue that governments will have to both ensure the freedom of people to come and go as they choose and not closely gear their immigration policy to perceived labour market shortages and requirements (Harris 1995).

Notes

1. "World system" theorists define capitalism in terms primarily of the market, under conditions (merchant capital, mercantilism, European colonialism) that can be traced back to the fifteenth century. Marxists, on the other hand take the institution of private property as well as both the market and the state as pillars of the capitalist system, but take as the sine qua non of capitalism the social institution of wage labour. At issue here is the origins of capitalism, which in the one case is traced back to the fifteenth century, and in the other to the nineteenth century — to the enclosure of the commons and the formation of a class of wage labourers.

2. Capitalism long ago evolved "into a world system of colonial oppression and of financial strangulation of the overwhelming majority of the population of the world by a handful of exceptionally rich and powerful states which plunder the whole world" (Lenin, Preface to the French and German editions of *Imperialism, the Highest Stage of Capitalism*).

3. For example, all of the members of the royal family and the great Whig families of England made fortunes out of this miserable trade in human flesh, fortunes which they invested in the construction of canals and coal mines. Those who made their fortunes on the slave trade included Sir Isaac Newton, the famous scientist; Sir John Vanburgh, architect, playwright and founder of King's College, Cambridge; The Earl of Halifax, founder of the Bank of England; Francis Baring, founder of Baring's Bank; and William Beckfort (1709–1770), Lord Mayor of London and the richest plantation owner (Hardy 2009). A 1720s list of shareholders of the slave-trading South Sea Company names most of the 462 members of the House of Commons and half the members of the House of Lords.

4. The invention of the steam engine, and with it the railways and steam-ships, made international migration a realistic proposition on a large scale. Consequently, according to Brown (1995), by 1840, 70,000 people emigrated each year from Britain and by the mid-1850s this number had doubled. Most of these emigrants went to Canada, Australia, New Zealand and the U.S. As a result, by 1871 Britain became a net exporter of people and, with a few notable exceptions, continued to be so throughout each successive decade right up to 1990 (Brown 1995).

5. On this see Sunkel and Infante (2010) and the World Bank 2008.

6. However, to place these migration flows in perspective they pale in comparison to the huge waves of migration stemming from conditions of industrial capitalism in the nineteenth century — in what in retrospect can be seen as the first era of globalization, from the second half of the nineteenth century to the First World War. In the 40 years leading up to WWI, migration increased the New World labour force by a third and reduced the European labour force by an eighth. While the total number of migrants today (232 million) constitutes just 3 percent of the global population, in the nineteenth century they represented 10 percent (Hardy 2009).

7. Structural adjustment programs based on the triad of trade openness, deregulation and privatization have been a main driver for the imposition of neoliberal restructuring policies. These programs have been promoted and imposed by the sister institutions of the Bretton Woods system — the International Monetary Fund (IMF), the World Bank and World Trade Organisation.

8. It is worth emphasizing that this ideology veils the fact that rather than a "free market" what the contemporary capitalist world system is actually about is that a handful of large MNCs, together with the imperial states and the financial institutions under their governance, control the lion's share of global trade.

References

Alden, E. 2012. "Immigration and Border Control." *CATO Journal* 32, 1: 107–23

American Immigration Law Foundation. 2002. "ESL Education Helps Immigrants Integrate." <www.ailf.org/ipc/policy_reports+2--2_ESL. asp>.

Blackburn, Robin. 1998. *The Making of New World Slavery: From the Baroque to the Modern, 1492–1800.* London: Verso.

Brown, Ruth. 1995. "Racism and Immigration in Britain." *International Socialism Journal* (Autumn).

Cohen, Robin. 2006. *Migration and Its Enemies: Global Capital, Migrant Labour and the Nation-State.* Aldershot: Ashgate.

____. 1987. *The New Helots: Migrants in the International Division of Labour.* Hants, UK: Gower Publishing.

Cypher, James, and Raúl Delgado Wise. 2011. *Mexico's Economic Dilemma: The Developmental Failure of Neoliberalism.* Maryland: Rowman & Littlefield.

____. 2007. "The Strategic Role of Mexican Labor under NAFTA: Critical Perspectives on Current Economic Integration." *The Annals of the American Academy of Political and Social Science* 615: 120–42.

Delgado Wise, R., H. Márquez and R. Puentes. 2013. "Reframing the Debate on Migration, Development and Human Rights." *Population, Space and Place* 19, 4: 430–43.

Geiger, M., and A. Pécoud (eds.). 2010. *The Politics of International Migration Management: Migration, Minorities and Citizenship.* Basingstoke: Palgrave Macmillan.

Hanson, G.H. 2007. "The Economic Logic of Illegal Immigration." Washington: Council on Foreign Relations Special Report.

Hardy, Jane. 2009. "Migration, Migrant Workers and Capitalism." *International Socialism* 22 (March 31).

Harris, Nigel. 1995. *The New Untouchables: Immigration and the New World Order.* Penguin.

INEGI (Instituto Nacional de Estadística, Geografía e Informática). 2014. "Estadística mensual sobre establecimientos con programa IMMEX." <http://www.inegi.org.mx/inegi/contenidos/notasinformativas/est_immex/ni-immex.pdf>.

Lenin, V.I. 1917. *Imperialism, the Highest Stage of Capitalism.* <http://www.fordham.edu/halsall/mod/1916lenin-imperialism.html>.

Marx, Karl. 1954 [1867]. *Capital: A Critique of Political Economy,* Vol. 1. Moscow: Progress Publishers. <http://www.marxists.org/archive/marx/works/download/pdf/Capital-Volume-I.pdf>.

Mendes Pereira, João Márcio. 2014. "Banco Mundial: dos bastidores años 50 de Bretton Woods (1942–1994)." *Revista Topoi,* Rio de Janeiro, 15, 29: 527–56.

Northrup, David. 1995. *Indentured Labour in the Age of Imperialism.* Cambridge: Cambridge University.

Passel, Jeffrey, and D'Vera Cohn. 2014. "Unauthorized Immigrant Totals Rise in 7 States, Fall in 14. Decline in Those from Mexico Fuels Most State Decreases." Pew Research Hispanic Trends Project. <http://www.pewhispanic.org/2014/11/18/unauthorized-immigrant-totals-rise-in-7-states-fall-in-14/>.

Potts, Lydia. 1990. *The World Labour Market: A History of Migration.* London: Zed Books.

Rodney, Walter. 1972. *How Europe Underdeveloped Africa.* London & Dar-es-Salaam: Bogle-L'Ouverture Publications.

Saxe-Fernández, John, and Omar Núñez. 2001. "Globalización e Imperialismo: La transferencia de Excedentes de América Latina." In Saxe-Fernández et al. *Globalización, Imperialismo y Clase Social*. Buenos Aires/México: Editorial Lúmen.

Strikwerda, Carl, and Camille Guerin-Gonzales. 1993. "Introduction." In *The Politics of Immigrant Workers, Labor Activism and Migration in the World Economy Since 1830*. New York and London: Holmes & Meier.

Sunkel, Osvaldo, and Ricardo Infante. 2010. *Hacia un Desarrollo Inclusivo: El Caso de Chile*. Santiago, Chile: CEPAL.

Tinker, Hugh. 1974. *A New System of Slavery: The Export of Indian Labour Overseas, 1830–1920*. Oxford University Press.

Williams, Eric. 1944. *Capitalism and Slavery*. Richmond, VA: University of North Carolina Press.

World Bank. 2008. *World Development Report 2008. Agriculture for Development*. Washington, DC: World Bank.

Chapter 4

The Political Economy of International Labour Migration

To fully understand the dynamics of labour migration it is important to remember that under capitalism the means of production,
including the worker's own labour power, which is exchanged
against capital for a living wage, is converted into commodities,
i.e., goods produced for sale on the market. But labour is not just a
commodity like any other; it has the capacity to create value greater
than itself (surplus value), which is appropriated by the owners of
the means of production, the capitalist class. To all appearances
the free exchange of labour power for a wage is an exchange of
equivalents, providing both capitalists and workers a fair return
on their respective contributions to social production. However,
workers do not receive a wage that equals the value they produce
(i.e., the product of their labour) but rather they receive only the
reproduction costs of their labour power, or as Marx put it, "the
value of the necessaries required to produce, develop, maintain,
and perpetuate the labouring power" (1969: 18). The difference,
surplus value, is appropriated by the capitalist as private profit,
which is used to accumulate capital. This fundamental premise to
the analysis of capitalism is presented by Marx in the first volume
of *Capital* (1954 [1967]). In the first section of Chapter 17 of
Capital, Marx states:

> There are, besides, two other factors that enter into the
> determination of the value of labour-power. One, the ex-
> penses of developing that power, which expenses vary with
> the mode of production; the other, its natural diversity, the
> difference between the labour-power of men and women, of
> children and adults. The employment of these different sorts
> of labour-power, an employment which is, in its turn, made
> necessary by the mode of production, makes a great differ-

ence in the cost of maintaining the family of the labourer, and in the value of the labour-power of the adult male. (362)

The New International Division of Labour

The neoliberal era opened a new phase in the history of contemporary capitalism based on the exploitation of an apparently unlimited supply of surplus and thus cheap labour generated in the capitalist development of agriculture and other sectors of the economy subjected to the destructive impacts of neoliberal restructuring (see Chapter 2 on the dynamics of this process). In the immediate postwar era of the old developmentalism this supply of rural labour, offered by small landholding peasant farmers who were pushed off the farm and both forced and encouraged to migrate to the cities in the search of greater economic opportunities, was used to fuel an industrialization process, leading to the formation of nuclei of modern capitalist economies in the urban centres. The 1970s, a time in which the world capitalist system was in crisis, saw many MNCs shift their labour-intensive operations to the urban centres in the underdeveloped countries of the global south in order to take advantage of their reserves of cheap labour.

This strategy, adopted and widely used by corporate executives who were concerned only with the bottom line, was facilitated by the imposition of structural adjustment programs in many countries of the global south, particularly in Latin America. These programs had a double impact. On the one hand, they meant a dismantling of the domestic economic apparatus, and on the other they created structural conditions that opened a pathway for MNCs to shift some of their operations to peripheral regions in order to profit from their abundant reserves of cheap and flexible labour. In this new arrangement governments were forced to compete for capital and technology and, in particular, for the new jobs that these corporations were expected to provide. To attract capital in the form of foreign direct investment, these governments offered to provide free enterprise tax-free zones in which corporations could set up assembly plants, import computer-processed products and spare parts to produce automobiles and electronics equipment and consumer goods for the world market, using cheap manufacturing labour (costing from one-seventh to one-tenth of the price in the United States).

At the same time as foreign investors and MNCs were invited into some countries on the periphery of the world capitalist system — especially in Latin America and the Caribbean — a number of governments in Southeast Asia (South Korea, Taiwan, Singapore, Hong Kong) pursued a strategy pioneered by Japan, which was to provide substantive support the production of manufactures for the world market. The combination of this industrial policy (state planning, industrialization and export promotion) with the strategy by multinationals to relocate their labour-intensive production operations closer to overseas supplies of cheap labour, resulted in what development economists termed "an economic miracle" (rapid growth on the periphery of the world system) and a "new international division of labour" (NIDL), a result of the transformations generated in the global economy by the neoliberal model.

One of the features of this NIDL, in large measure the unintended consequence of the search by the MNCs for ways to lower labour costs, was the emergence in the world economy of a bloc of "newly industrializing countries" (NICs) (Frobel, Heinrichs and Kreye 1980). Most of these NICs were in Southeast Asia — the first tier or generation comprising South Korea, Taiwan, Singapore and Hong Kong, followed by China and India, and a second generation that eventually formed the Association of Southeast and Asian Nations (ASEAN), a powerful new economic and trading bloc.

The end result of these and other forces of change operating in the sphere of international economic relations was the formation of new global capitalist world economy characterized by the following:

1. a new world order of neoliberal globalization: a set of rules and financial architecture based on the Washington consensus regarding the declared virtues and principles of free market capitalism — the free flow of investment capital, tradable goods and services — in a global economy dominated by monopoly capital[1];

2. uneven development of the forces of production, including the

emergence of new national centres of capital accumulation, the emergence of China as an economic power (now the largest economy in the world, overtaking the U.S. towards the end of 2014) and persistence of a north-south division in the wealth of nations;

3. a new international division of labour, resulting from the shift by the large MNCs of their labour-intensive operations to some countries on the periphery in order to take advantage of their large reserves of cheap labour;

4. industrialization of some countries on the periphery (particularly China, India and the countries that comprise ASEAN), having been converted into manufacturing export platforms; others, particularly Mexico, converted into exporters of labour[2]; at the same time many countries, particularly in South America and Africa, which are not part of this NIDL, continue to export raw materials and primary commodities in exchange for goods manufactured in both the centre of the world capitalist system and "newly industrializing countries" such as China;

5. new economic and political alliances and trading blocs, including ALBA, MERCOSUR, the Andean Pact and UNASUR in South America, CARICOM in the Caribbean, NAFTA in North America, and ASEAN. A major feature of this new structure is the formation of BRICS, a loose but potentially powerful — in world market terms — association of middle and emerging economic powers formed by Brazil, Russia, India and China;

6. a new global labour market fuelled by a continuing process of agrarian transformation in the global south and the expansion of a global reserve army of surplus labour as a consequence of this process; and, in line with what Lenin had described as a "special feature of imperialism" (the most advanced state of capitalism to that date); and

7. relative decline in emigration from the imperialist countries and the increase in immigration into these countries from the more backward countries where lower wages are paid, reinforcing a worldwide trend towards the weakening of the negotiation power and the living conditions of workers.

Formation of a Global Labour Market

Marx wrote about the formation of an industrial reserve army as an inevitable outcome of the capitalist development process, which he theorised in terms of the workings of a "general law of capital accumulation" as a necessary part of the capitalist organization of work.[3] As he saw it, the proletarianization of the direct producers tends to expand at a rate faster than the labour market can absorb, resulting in what economists today would describe as "structural unemployment," a condition in which the supply of labour power exceeds the demand for it.[4] Given the constant pressures on capital for technological innovation and conversion of the labour process — replacing live labour with dead labour or technology — a propensity towards structural under- and unemployment is built into the capitalist system. Thus, over time, a part of the working population will tend to become *surplus* to the requirements of capital accumulation.

Paradoxically, the larger the wealth of society, the larger the industrial reserve army. However, as Marx expands on the argument it also becomes clear that, depending on the state of the economy in the context of an inherent trend towards uneven development, the reserve army of labour will either expand or contract, alternately being absorbed or expelled from the employed workforce. Thus Marx concludes that "relative surplus-population is ... the pivot upon which the law of demand and supply of labour works." The availability of labour influences wage rates, and the larger the unemployed labour force, the more this forces down wage rates; conversely, if there are plenty jobs available and unemployment is low, this tends to raise the average level of wages.

The labour market thus encompasses and engages what Marx described as "the army of labour" and a "reserve army" of workers whose labour power was surplus to the requirements of the system. The army of labour consists in those working-class people employed in average or better-than-average jobs — what the International Labour Organization (ILO) today describes as "decent work." Of course, not every one in the working class gets one of these jobs. There are four other work situations and conditions in which members of the working class might find themselves: the "stagnant pool," the "floating reserve," the "latent reserve" and "immiseration" or poverty, a condition in which workers are no longer able to meet their basic needs. This condition relates to workers who are unable to meet even the minimal requirements of the labour market (basic literacy, etc.) or are forced to abandon it altogether due to some disability, mental illness or another reason. Marx characterized these people, some of whom would inevitably turn towards crime as a means of subsistence, as the "lumpenproletariat") (Duggan 2013). Mike Davis (2006) labels them in the current conjuncture of world capitalist development as the "outcast proletariat."

In this understanding of the labour market, the stagnant pool part of the relative surplus population or reserve army consists of marginalized workers with "extremely irregular employment." Stagnant pool jobs are characterized by below average remuneration or pay, dangerous working conditions, job insecurity and social exclusion (Pochmann 2004; Roldán 2013). Those stuck in the stagnant pool have jobs and are thus included in the labour force participation statistics as "employed." The floating reserve army are workers who used to have good jobs but are now out of work, a situation described today by labour economists as "conjunctural unemployment." The *latent* part of the reserve army consists of that segment of the population that is not yet fully integrated into the capitalist production process. In Marx's day, this would apply to those who were searching for wage employment in industry but still to some extent dependent on subsistence agriculture. In the contemporary conjuncture of capitalist development, or "modern times" in common parlance, it applies predominantly to the masses of people coming or migrating from the "planet of slums" in underdeveloped countries, where they survive largely by working "on their own account" in the informal sector or by non-monetary means.

By all accounts this global reserve army today — dispossessed yet locked out of the productive economy — has reached gigantic proportions. Stimulated by the dismantling of the Soviet Union and the incorporation of China and India into the capitalist world economy and the implementation of structural reforms (including privatization and the flexibilization of labour) in the global south, the supply of labour available to capital over the last two decades more than doubled, from 1.5 to 3.3 billion, in what Richard Freeman (2006) calls the "great doubling." Yet those uprooted and dispossessed have not been absorbed into formal employment. The ILO reported that at the end of the century, one-third of the world's economically active population was unemployed — that is, idle labour, a global reserve army of the unemployed, what Davis has termed the "outcast proletariat" found in the world's megacities.

From Pax Britannica to Pax Americana

For about fifteen years, from the onset of the Great Depression in 1930 to the end of the Second World War, the world capitalist system was in crisis, a situation reflected in reduced rates of economic growth at the centre of the system, high levels of unemployment and a reduction in the levels of both international trade and international migration. But by the end of the Second World War, the situation had significantly changed. Free market capitalism was discredited and replaced with a system that combined elements of both capitalism and socialism — a "mixed economy" as it was termed. The capitalist system in the U.S. had recovered its economic dynamism and was restructured under the aegis of the state, and the U.S. emerged as an economic superpower, disposing of almost one-half of world industrial production capacity and 80 percent of the world's gold reserves in bullion and enormous pools of investment capital accumulated over the course of the war, which had served U.S. capital as a vast engine of economic growth.

Given its status as a capitalist superpower, the U.S. took immediate steps to assert its economic and political power and establish its hegemony over the system, converting itself into the leader of the "free world" — the forces of economic and political freedom, which had won a major victory over European fascism. The U.S. mobilized its economic and political power in the construction of a new world order, a system designed to reactivate the capital accumulation process on a global scale.

Whereas the domestic market had been the major engine of economic growth — an economic expansion fuelled by a steady rise in wages and the purchasing power capacity of workers and the middle class — the aim of U.S. policymakers and the officials of an emerging imperial state was to reactivate a process of capital accumulation (and expand U.S. production) by means of international trade, creating overseas markets for U.S. capital in the form of U.S.-based MNCs. And indeed, in the subsequent "golden age of capitalism" (two decades of sustained economic growth across the system), growth in U.S. international trade exceeded by a factor of two the growth of the GDP, and U.S.-based MNCs increased their command of the world market. By the end of the 1970s U.S. capital in the form of multinational corporations achieved a dominant position, accounting for over 40 percent of the 100 biggest MNCs operating in the world system.

However, the dominance of U.S. industrial capital in the world market was not necessarily reflected in the U.S.'s balance of payments. While the U.S. maintained a positive balance in its trade with countries on the south of the global divide, especially Latin America and the Caribbean, by the end of the 1970s the U.S. was locked into a major war for the global market with its major rivals — ironically, Germany and Japan. It turns out that the U.S. state was perforce constrained to use the balance on its trade account with countries in Latin America and the Caribbean to offset a growing imbalance on its trade account with its rival capitalist powers.

The Structure of the Global Labour Market

A major impetus for the construction of the new world order in the 1980s was the search for a way out of a systemic crisis of overproduction, a crisis that was reflected in stagnant or sluggish rates of economic growth and productivity growth, falling profits and a high and increasing rate of unemployment in the labour market. The assumption was that the new world order would create conditions for a renewed process of capital accumulation on a global scale, including the removal of restrictions on the free flow of investment capital and barriers to the free movement of goods.

One outcome of this process (removing the barriers to free trade and the free movement of capital by means of "structural reform" of national policy) was the destruction of productive forces in both industry and agriculture. Another outcome, in part a response to this outcome, was an acceleration in the process of outmigration from the rural areas and the extension of this process overland (primarily from Central America and Mexico) and overseas on a south-north axis of international labour migration. In fact, according to the World Bank (2011), 156 million of the existing 214 million migrants in 2010, or 72 percent, come from the periphery of the world system in the global south.

This migration process can be referred as the direct export of labour in order to differentiate it from the export of the *maquiladora* assembly plants in Mexico and elsewhere in Latin America and Asia, which relates to an indirect or disembodied form of labour exportation that does not entail international migration. This characterization attempts to capture the true essence of *maquiladora* exports, given the overwhelming incorporation of imported inputs (between 80 and 90 percent) and the fact that labour is by far its main domestic input (Delgado Wise and Márquez 2007; Delgado Wise and Cypher 2007). As for the direct export of the labour force, via labour migration, it implies a transfer of the anticipated future benefits that arise from the costs of training and social reproduction of the emigrating workers. It has been demonstrated — with empirical data based on U.S. and Mexican official sources — that these costs are not compensated for by the inflow of migrant remittances, which economists at the World Bank argue constitute a potential source of development finance (Delgado Wise, Márquez and Rodríguez 2004). In demographic terms, labour migration results in the loss and south-north transfer of a fundamental productive human resource for national development — what has been described as "the demographic dividend."

This is particularly the case for countries on the periphery of the world capitalist system that are in an advanced stage of a demographic shift of the population from the countryside to the urban centres, when declining birth rates create a large working-age population relative to the pre-working-age and retired seniors. In a profound sense, this transfer implies the loss of the most important potential resource for capital accumulation in the country of origin: its labour force. Furthermore, the export of highly skilled labour exacerbates this problem by seriously reducing the sending country's capacity to innovate for its own benefit and drive its own technology-intensive development projects.

Global Labour Arbitrage
within the Neoliberal Restructuring Process

A key element for understanding the role played by labour markets in the process of capital accumulation at a global scale is the notion of labour arbitrage. In order to understand this notion, it is necessary to transcend the level of abstraction at which the notion of the value of labour-power is constructed by Marx in *Capital* — "capital in general" (Moseley 1995) — and to remember that wages, or the cost of reproducing the labour force, has two dimensions: one material and the other cultural, and that these are defined historically and nationally, depending on the type of labour in question. In his text *Value, Price and Profit*, Marx notes: "Besides this mere physical element the value of labour is in every country determined to by a traditional standard of life. It is not merely the physical life, but it is the satisfaction of certain wants springing from the social conditions in which people are placed and reared up" (1969: 27).

In the wage differences between countries and within them, an important element emphasized by Marx is the wage pressure exerted by the reserve army of labour. Another point highlighted by Marx, which reinforces the recognition of wage differentials between countries, is the following: "By comparing the standard wages or values of labour in different countries, and by comparing them in different historical epochs of the same country, you will find that the value of labour itself is not a fixed but variable, even supposing the values of all other commodities to remain constant" (1969: 28). Thus, the costs of subsistence and reproduction vary widely depending on historical, cultural and national conditions, and therefore wages between countries can vary widely as well.

What is important to emphasize here is that throughout the long history of capitalism, and in particular with the advent of imperialism in the advanced stage of capitalism, the asymmetries between countries tend to grow and expand. Under neoliberalism, this trend is exacerbated. In turn the explosive growth in the global reserve army of labour and its unequal spatial distribution have generated and deepened the enormous wage differentials between countries.

Although we do not have a detailed systematic structural analysis of the differential wage rates and working conditions in countries across the world that constitute this market, Table 4.1 provides an illustrative pattern for a number of countries. It points to a pattern of dynamic international migrant labour flows, which reflect both national differences in wage rates and working conditions, and the workings of market forces, government migration policies and the geoeconomics of capital.[5]

Table 4.1 Labour Cost Differentials: Average Wages for Production Workers, Selected Countries (2009) (US$ per hour)

Indonesia	0.70
China	1.27
India	1.68
Thailand	2.78
Mexico	3.28
South Korea	5.47
Spain	13.01
France	14.29
U.K.	20.01
Canada	21.39
Japan	22.61
U.S.	25.34
Germany	34.46

Source: Boston Consulting Group

The rules of the neoliberal world order of free market capitalism, which was installed in the early 1980s, liberated the "forces of economic freedom" from the regulatory constraints of the welfare-development state. Not only did this freedom lead to the penetration of capital in the global south in the form of large-scale foreign investors looking for economic opportunities (profits) in accessing markets, cheap labour, raw materials and natural resources for export and in purchasing public assets, but it also led to a process of financialization, which refers to the ascendancy of finance capital over other forms of capital (Bello 2005: 101).

One outcome of this financialization is an increased propensity towards crisis, which can be attributed to the unimpeded growth of fictitious capital based on untrammelled greed and speculative investments — investing in possible outcomes that have nothing to do with production — such as variations in the exchange value of different currencies, the future price of commodities, derivatives etc. It is estimated that in the 1970s, at least 75 percent of investments were productive in the sense that they were invested in and led to the expansion of production. But by the end of the 1990s, after less than two decades of financialization, it was estimated that less than 5 percent of the economic transactions in the world's capital markets had any connection to the real economy whatsoever.

Another outcome of financialization has been the increased concentration of productive capital and the monopolization of finance, production, services and trade, leaving every major global industry to be dominated by a small number of large MNCs.[6] In the expansion of their operations, the agents of corporate capitalism created a global process of production, finance, distribution and investment that has allowed them to seize the strategic and profitable segments of peripheral economies and appropriate the economic surplus produced at enormous social and environmental costs. Thus, while labour in this world was subject to increasing global competition, market discipline and austerity measures in public policy, it confronted an increasingly concentrated capital backed up by the state, fundamentally altering the balance of class power in the favour of capital.

In the world economy, monopoly capital in the form of the multinational corporation has become more than ever the central player.[7] Through a process of mega-mergers and strategic alliances, this fraction of global capital (versus the capitalists that finance these operations and run the capital markets) has reached unparalleled levels of concentration: the top five hundred largest MNCs now dispose of between 35–40 percent of world income (Foster, McChesney and Jonna 2011a). However, even more important is the fact that in the neoliberal era monopoly capital has undergone a profound restructuring process based on the "comparative advantage" provided to some capitalists over others by a process of "global labour arbitrage."

This process of global labour arbitrage — taking advantage of wage differentials in peripheral regions — is accomplished through global networks of monopoly capital (GNMC) which outsource and subcontract a production chain that provides the MNCs opportunities to make super-profits from the exploitation and the super-exploitation of abundant and cheap labour. The GNMCs also extract (or pillage) and export unprocessed natural resources in the form of ground rent (Márquez and Delgado Wise 2011). This turn toward GNMCs has been impressive: "[the] top one hundred global corporations had shifted their production more decisively to their foreign affiliates [mainly in the south], which now account for close to 60 percent of their total assets and employment and more than 60 percent of their global sales" (UNCTAD 2010). This constitutes a "new 'nomadism' [that] has emerged within the system of global production, with locational decisions determined largely by where labour is cheapest" (Foster, McChesney and Jonna 2011a: 18). An important feature of this process is that least 40 percent of global trade, including subcontracting and intra-firm trade, is associated with outsourcing operations (Andreff 2009) and that it includes an estimated 85 million workers who are directly employed in assembly plants and over 3500 export processing zones established in 130 countries, mostly in the global south (McKinsey 2012).

This restructuring strategy has transformed the global geography of production to the point that now most of the world's industrial employment (over 70 percent) is located in the global south (Foster, McChesney and Jonna 2011b).

However, the global labour arbitrage system does not only implicate an industrial labour force of production workers and operatives. It includes a system for accessing sources of highly qualified labour needed for the production of technology- and knowledge-intensive goods and services required by the new globalized knowledge economy and also for research and development, to fulfil the need for constant cutting-edge innovation. The competitive pressures for constant technological innovation in the new globalized economy is intense, as is competition for "brain power," leading to the brain drain from the south to the north, a haemorrhage of human capital of such proportions as to constitute one of the greatest obstacles faced by many underdeveloped countries in their quest for national development.

To ensure access to sources of the capital embodied in human labour, corporations have resorted to a variety of tactics, including the internationalization of their knowledge production and innovation systems, and opening up to and sharing knowledge-intensive corporate functions with a growing network of external partners, such as suppliers, clients, subcontractors, universities, etc. to create "ecosystems" of innovation (OECD 2008). Other strategies include the creation of scientific cities such as Silicon Valley in the U.S. and the new "Silicon Valleys" established in peripheral or emerging regions, principally in Asia — where collective synergies are created to accelerate innovation processes (Sturgeon 2003).

However, many MNCs tend to stick to the tried and true "traditional" methods of ensuring a monopoly over technological innovation and knowledge production. These include (1) appropriating the products of scientific endeavours through the acquisition of patents; (2) financing the production of new knowledge by partners in the private and public sectors; and (3) recruiting highly skilled workers, particularly in the areas of science and engineering, from universities and research centres in the global south, through sponsored immigration, institutional partnerships, outsourcing and offshoring (Batelle 2012). Although some authors point towards a "new geography of innovation" and "scientific *maquiladoras*" based on outsourcing, studies sponsored by UNCTAD show that governments in the north have implemented immigration policies designed to attract highly qualified workers from the global south, with the resulting brain drain.

Development Dynamics of a South-North Brain Drain

For a glimpse into the development implications of the concerted efforts of capitalists and the state in the global north to monopolize the brain power of societies in the global south, consider the following facts, presented by Fidel Castro in one of his famous "reflections" ("The Brain Drain"), which was published on July 17, 2007. Castro reports on a Reuters press dispatch (May 3, 2006), titled "African brain drain deprives Africa of vital talent." The dispatch read "it is estimated that some 20,000 skilled professionals are leaving the continent every year, depriving Africa of the doctors, nurses, teachers and engineers it needs to break a cycle of poverty and underdevelopment." Quoting a report from the World Bank, the dispatch also reported that "stymied by conflict, poverty, lethal diseases and corruption, much of Africa is in no position to compete with richer countries that promise higher salaries, better working conditions and political stability." In regard to these and other reports on the "brain drain," Fidel Castro observed: "The brain drain deals a double blow to weak economies, which not only lose their best human resources and the money spent training them, but then have to pay an estimated $5.6 billion a year to employ expatriates." One of these reports, titled "International Migration, Remittances and the Brain Drain," by the World Bank in October 2005, yielded the following: "In the last 40 years, more than 1.2 million professionals from Latin America and the Caribbean have emigrated to the United States, Canada and the United Kingdom" (Ozden and Schiff 2005: 10). The report adds that "an average of 70 scientists a day has emigrated from Latin America in the course of 40 years."

In the period, 2000–2012, the U.S. alone was the recipient of 1.5 million highly qualified university educated migrants (RIMD 2015) from the global south, predominantly from Latin America and the Caribbean. In 2012 there were 857,268 Mexicans who had migrated to the U.S. with a university degree in hand prior to their migration; 981,581 from the Caribbean; 951,737 from South America and 423,462 from Central America; altogether over three million highly qualified university educated migrants from Latin America and the Caribbean, whose education and professional formation was entirely paid for by their country of origin — a mass of human capital and brain power lost to their countries of origin (RIMD 2015: 11). A study sponsored by the World Bank (Ozden and Schiff 2005: 10) found that by 2000 many Central American and island states in the Caribbean had lost over 50 percent of their university-educated citizens.

This brain drain phenomenon can be seen as a paradigmatic example of what has been conceptualized as the "development of underdevelopment," an economic structure in which economically backward or relatively poor countries on the periphery of the world capitalist system contribute to the "economic development" of societies at the centre while the societies on the periphery are impoverished and underdeveloped as a result. A number of clear examples of this situation can be found in the Caribbean islands, which report the world's highest brain drain. It transpires that in some of these islands, eight of every ten university graduates have left their native country, a brain drain of enormous proportions with a devastating impact on the possibilities and prospects for economic and social development. Not only have a number of countries, particularly small nations in Africa, the Caribbean and Central America, as a result of migration lost over 30 percent of their population with higher education but this loss represents nothing less than a haemorrhage of society's built-up stock vital human resources, a depletion of the human capital needed for their development.

A report published by the ILO and reviewed by Castro points out that the number of scientists and engineers who abandon their native country and emigrate to an industrialized nation is about one-third of the number of those who stay in their native country, a significant depletion of that country's indispensable human resource reserves. The ILO report also maintains that the migration of students is a precursor of the brain drain. In this regard, the Organization for Economic Cooperation and Development (OECD) reported that at the beginning of the millennium, around 1.5 million foreign students pursued higher studies in member states and that of these more than half were from non-OECD countries. Of this total, nearly half a million studied in the U.S., one quarter of a million in the U.K. and nearly 200,000 in Germany. Between 1960 and 1990, the U.S. and Canada received more than one million professional immigrants and experts from underdeveloped countries. These facts and figures, Castro notes, significant as they are, represent but "a pale reflection of the [broader] tragedy" visited upon underdeveloped countries by the wealthy advanced capitalist countries in pursuit of their economic interests.

The promotion of the immigration of highly qualified labour migrants from the underdeveloped countries of the global south is an important element of public policy in advanced capitalist countries. For example, the American Competitiveness in the Twenty-First Century Act, approved by the U.S. Congress in 2000 increased the temporary work visa (H-1B) allotment from 65,000 to 115,000 in the 2000 fiscal year and then to 195,000 for fiscal years

2001 through 2003. The aim of this increase in the visa cap — and similar measures were promulgated by the U.K., Germany, Canada and Australia — was to encourage the entry into the U.S. of highly qualified immigrants who could occupy positions in the technology sector of the burgeoning knowledge economy. Although the visa cap was reduced to 65,000 in the 2005 fiscal year, the flow of professionals towards the U.S. has remained steady ever since.

The relentless plundering of brain power in the countries of the global south, Castro concluded, has a significant impact on the development prospects of countries on both sides of the global divide, contributing substantively to economic development in the north and inhibiting this development in the south. In these countries the migration policy and actions taken by governments in the north have a profoundly negative impact, dismantling and weakening programs aimed at the accumulation of human capital, a vital productive resource which is needed, as Castro argued, for these countries "to rise from the depths of underdevelopment." The advance of capitalism in the north, he added, is "not limited to the transfer of capital; it also entails the import of grey matter, which nips a country's nascent intelligence and future at the bud."

Contemporary Dynamics
of the International Migrant Labour Market

One of the main engines of capitalist development is cheap labour. The cost of labour, reflected in variable yet "structured" wage rates in different countries, can be affected by government intervention and tax policies but in the global economy to an important degree reflects the impact of a corporate-driven strategy regarding the global supply and demand of labour. Thus, capitalist employers are often in a position to take full advantage of the massive oversupply of labour relative to demand, shown in growing levels of unemployment the world over. But given the role assigned to global labour arbitrage, expansion of the global reserve army of labour has occurred most dramatically in the global south, where 73 percent of this "reserve army" for the global labour market or workforce can be found (Ghose, Maji and Ernst 2008).

Migrant workers are especially useful as part of the reserve army of labour because they can be easily expelled when no longer needed. And the use of migrant workers also allows the receiver country to externalize the costs of renewing the labour force. The state uses migrant workers to fill gaps in the labour market and to create downward pressures on wages without having to pay for the production and reproduction costs of this labour.

The size of this global reserve army of labour is dialectically related to the prevalence of low wages, a long-term trend towards the relative reduction in the value of labour-power (the purchasing power of the wage) and a chronic undersupply of "decent" employment, which characterizes contemporary capitalism. Under these conditions, a global oversupply of labour has resulted in a scaling down of the global wage structure and an increase in overall job insecurity. For example, according to ILO estimates, the number of workers in conditions of labour insecurity rose to 1.5 billion in 2010 — encompassing more than half of the world's labour force — with 630 million receiving a wage of less than US$2 per day, and nearly half of those finding themselves in situations of extreme poverty (ILO 2011). At the same time the number of the unemployed both in the north and south continues to rise, leading to class conflict over austerity measures in the north and growing pressures to emigrate in the south.

Under the Washington consensus regarding the virtues of free market capitalism (neoliberal "structural reform" in public policy) labour markets have been restructured and the working class reconfigured in the following ways:

1. *The creation of a dispersed and vulnerable proletariat available to global networks of monopoly capital.* The global production and value chains (the MNCs) that link the operating units of the world capitalist system to the workers, who, on one end of these chains, create or add value to the final product, and to the consumers, at the other end of these chains, are located in the strategic and most profitable sectors of global production — manufacturing, financial and technology high-end computer-mediated/information-rich services, fossil and bio-fuels, metals and minerals, and agriculture.

The neoliberal restructuring of labour markets has dismantled labour protection and imposed a new labour culture based on competitiveness, creating a regime of employment insecurity characterized by labour "flexibility" and the permanent threat of layoffs. Outsourcing stands out as a corporate management strategy for reducing labour costs. Another is the hiring of migrant workers, who are easier to exploit because they are often desperate and willing to work under insecure and poorly paid conditions, and in addition often have no experience with unions. This new proletariat is forced to endure high levels of exploitation in order to access a source of income. Needless to add, these workers tend to be alienated from any sense of class belonging and their place in the social structure, thus weakening the social bonds that hold working people together.

Under these conditions migrant workers have no human referent regarding their exploiters — only a faceless, mobile and deterritorialized corporate entity, which when necessary can quickly shift production to other factories. This abstract or impersonal form of capital undermines the development of any class consciousness regarding economic exploitation and the labour process, preventing workers from building the social relations that are necessary for cooperation and solidarity when confronting employers in the class struggle, and thus disempowering them (Sassen 1988: 39). The daily struggle to earn a livelihood consumes all of their energy.

2. *The covert proletarianization of the highly qualified scientific and technological worker*. The large MNCs have absorbed a global pool of scientific and technological labour, much of it sourced from the global south, into an innovation system that is protected by international property law (patents) and generates extraordinary profits. In this way the high-hanging fruits of technological progress are directly appropriated by monopoly capital.

Scientists and technologists constitute a privileged segment of the working class and do not normally view themselves as workers, but rather as part of the global ruling class and even promoters of social transformation inasmuch as their innovations affect everything from production patterns to the daily lives of ordinary people. However, a number of sociological studies have shown that workers in this highly qualified and skilled labour force have gradually lost, directly or covertly, their relative autonomy and control over the means of knowledge production and the tools of their labour (laboratories, research agendas, etc.). In this way, the labour power of a large swath of scientific and technological "workers" is subsumed by the large MNCs under conditions of alienated labour and the loss of class consciousness regarding the capitalist labour process. Under these conditions the MNCs drive the R&D agendas and appropriate the products of the research, i.e., acquire ownership rights over the products of intellectual labour.

3. *The real or disguised proletarianization of the peasantry.* A global agribusiness system dominated by large MNCs controls all stages of the productive, financial and trading processes, leaving practically no place for small-scale, family-owned or peasant agricultural production. Like other economic sectors, agribusiness employs subcontracting schemes that degrade peasant autonomy and entail both visible and covert forms of proletarianization with a high degree of insecurity. Through a process of accumulation by dispossession, the peasant economy of small-scale production for local food markets is destroyed and large-scale agribusiness production for export is expanded, leading to a loss of both food sovereignty and biodiversity, blocking public resources from being channelled into the peasant sector, and "freeing" the workforce from the land so that it can, in turn, be employed in precarious and unsafe conditions in other sectors — manufacturing, trade or services.

In order to subsist within the new institutional framework of neoliberal capitalism peasants are forced to either: (1) become a contract farmer, providing agribusiness corporations a supply of agro-food products while forcing the small landholding peasant farmers and agricultural producers to assume the risks and direct costs of production; (2) work for agribusiness under the wage relation rather than a product contract, even on lands they might have formerly owned; (3) migrate to the cities in search of precarious jobs, many of them offered by the large MNCs, and in areas such as the *maquiladora* industry zones; (4) seek to survive within the ranks of the lumpenproletariat, by engaging in the informal street market or criminal activities — and in some cases (especially in Mexico and Central America, but also Colombia and elsewhere in the Andes) entering the narco-economy; or (5) migrate abroad, in many cases to work in vulnerable social conditions and with poorly paid jobs. These processes of overt or covert proletarianization and sub-proletarianization exacerbate further the complex dynamics of semi-proletarianization already in place before the neoliberal onslaught.

Despite the social decomposition of the peasantry as a subaltern class formed in the interstices of the dominant capital-labour relation, it is worth noting that some of the most visible and consistent anti-globalization movements come precisely from the ranks of the peasantry and indigenous groups (e.g., Vía Campesina, the Zapatista Army of National Liberation in Mexico, CONEI in Ecuador and the Landless Workers Movement in Brazil), which suggests that many peasant organizations retain the social and geographic space necessary to develop counterhegemonic ideologies and bases of resistance (Petras and Veltmeyer 2013).

4.   *Semi-proletarianization of migrant workers.* Neoliberal capitalism has intensified the working of institutional and policy mechanisms of social exclusion and dispossession. The most evident result of this is the creation of a population that has no means of earning a living and whose livelihood is precarious at best. These social groups are forced to migrate domestically or internationally in order to access any source of income that will enable family subsistence. Migration in this context is far from being a free and voluntary movement; rather, it is a structural imperative. A wide range of social subjects are forced to move from their places of origin: peasants deprived of land or unable to make a living out of it; unemployed or poorly paid workers; young people with no employment prospects; professionals without access to social mobility; women lacking access to the labour market; skilled workers with few or no opportunities for work and income. Those who participate in forced migration are placed in relatively more adverse conditions than their native counterparts; they are turned into a proletariat, or sub-proletariat, which is forced to confront conditions of unemployment and job insecurity, social exclusion, wage discrimination, a loss of social and labour rights, precarious citizenship status, and criminalization. As a proletarian subclass they are often subjected to conditions of super-exploitation

and work conditions that hark back to pre-capitalist features of coercion and border on slavery.

5. *Expansion of the reserve army of labour.* With it comes an increase in new forms of poverty and the formation of an underclass of workers with little to no hope of finding any, let alone, decent work; some are disabled or incapacitated in different ways from entering the labour market under any conditions, constituting what Marx in a different context described as the "lumpenproletariat." These surplus workers suffer from the worst living and employment conditions and are found in the lowest social strata, a highly degraded segment of the global population. To survive, the poorest of the poor work on the margins of society and often beyond the margins of legality, forced into a life of petty crime, organized crime, human trafficking and prostitution. They also carry out activities in public spaces, working as beggars and mendicants, shoe-shiners, car watchers and washers, vendors and street musicians, among many other things. This category of workers also includes door-to-door vendors and informal street workers. The dysfunctional nature of their work, their detachment from the institutional framework of society and the discrimination they endure prevent them from developing a class identity.

6. *Subordination and resistance of the intellectual worker.* This segment of the working class — or, as some analysts have it, the petit bourgeoisie or new middle class — implicates individuals who are relatively detached from the class structure or have no fixed position within it and who are generally well-educated and often well paid for their services or contributions. Having no basic class interests to defend but a middle-class lifestyle to protect, workers in this category tend to be ideologically flexible and generally "for hire." However, even though they have to work for a living, their knowledge and skills place them in a different position in the labour market than most other workers. At the same time their need for work and their orientation towards a modern middle-class lifestyle means that large numbers of these well-educated and highly qualified intellectual workers end up working directly or indirectly for the captains of industry and finance, members of the capitalist class with the means to purchase their skills and knowledge. This has a major,

even decisive, impact on their ideological orientation and politics: as functionaries of the system they are generally well-paid for their services — so much so as to place them in a "contradictory class location" (the professional-management class) between the dominant bourgeoisie and the subordinate working class — as managers of capitalist enterprise and the ideological apparatus (production of the dominant ideology). In this position many intellectual workers end up working either directly or directly for big money, the capitalist class that owns most of the means of social production, controls the commanding heights of the economy and often has a commanding influence over the government of the day if not the state.[8]

Conclusion

One of the outcomes of the formation of a middle- and upper-middle class of intellectual workers is the creation and strengthening of a capitalist culture of consumerism and private enterprise, and the construction of what can well be described as a dominant ideology — ideas that serve to legitimate the workings of the operative economic system and to reproduce it. This ideology takes diverse forms, but revolves around the idea of freedom — the freedom of individuals to advance their self-interest and to take advantage of their economic opportunities. This idea has served to justify the imposition of a neoliberal model of free market capitalism and policy reform (privatization, deregulation, liberalization and globalization) on governments in the global south. It also serves to drive a singular form of thought regarding the need to liberate the "forces of freedom" (private enterprise, the market, electoral democracy) from the regulatory constraints of the welfare-development state. This ideology, including the idea that there is no alternative to capitalism (that history has come to an end), today dominates all of the institutions that make up the ideological apparatus — the education system and academe, the mass media and the political system of parliaments, governments and political parties. Through the working of these institutions these ideas have become so generalized and effective as to provide most people a "common sense" understanding of the world as they see and live it.

Another outcome of class formation in the world capitalist economy — which we elaborate as the central theme of this book — is the creation of a global labour market for highly qualified and skilled labour, which has fuelled a global migratory process based on a south-north flow of highly qualified and skilled workers from the periphery to the centre of the world capitalist system. The socio-economic and policy dynamics of this process, and its development implications both for the migrant-sending countries in the south and the migrant receiving countries in the north, are discussed above and again in Chapter 6.

In addition to legitimizing neoliberal policies that subject the societies in the underdeveloped world to destructive forces of contemporary capitalism and that subordinate governments to the economic interests of an emerging international capitalist class, the dominant ideology also serves to justify a system based on the exploitation of labour and a situation in which the lion's share of the global social product — the wealth of nations — is appropriated by the capitalist class, and the exceedingly heavy social and environmental costs of (capitalist) development are borne by the working class both in the south and the north.

This phenomenon — the uneven development of the forces of global production and the pervasive inequalities in the distribution of wealth and income — is both symptomatic and revealing in regard to the fundamental "contradiction" of capitalism. First, it is evident that the neoliberal model of free market capitalism has led to a sharpening of this contradiction, unleashing in the process forces that constitute a brutal and uncompromising attack on the living and working conditions of the working class. This process, marked by an intensification of asymmetries between countries and regions as well as unprecedented social polarization, and masked by the ideology of free market capitalism, has also produced what some see as a profound civilizational crisis. In the following chapter we explore one particular dimension of this crisis as it relates to migration in the capitalist development process.

Notes

1. This world order did not include the movement of people, or even of labour, a fundamental factor of global production.

2. Since the main domestic input in Mexico's "*maquiladora*-like" industrialized exports is labour, what the country actually "exports" is the most precious merchandise for capital accumulation: its workforce (Delgado and Marquez 2007).

3. Although the idea of the industrial reserve army of labour is closely associated with Marx, it was already in circulation in the British labour movement by the 1830s (Denning 2010). Frederick Engels (1962), in his classic study of the social condition of the English working class, wrote that "English manufacture must have, at all times save the brief periods of highest prosperity, an unemployed reserve army of labour, in order to produce the masses of goods required by the market in the liveliest months." The first mention of the reserve army of labour in Marx's writing occurs in a manuscript he wrote in 1847 but did not publish: "Big industry constantly requires a reserve army of unemployed workers for times of overproduction. The main purpose of the bourgeoisie in relation to the worker is, of course, to have the commodity labour as cheaply as possible, which is only possible when the supply of this commodity is as large as possible in relation to the demand for it, i.e., when the overpopulation is the greatest. Overpopulation is therefore in the interest of the bourgeoisie, and it gives the workers good advice that it knows to be impossible to carry out. Since capital only increases when it employs workers, the increase of capital involves an increase of the proletariat, and, as we have seen, according to the nature of the relation of capital and labour, the increase of the proletariat must proceed relatively even faster" (Marx, *Wages*, December 1847).

4. Prior to what Marx regarded as the start of the capitalist era in human history (the sixteenth century), structural unemployment on a mass scale rarely existed other than that caused by natural disasters and wars. In ancient societies, all people who could work necessarily had to work, otherwise they would starve; a slave or a serf by definition could not become "unemployed." In fact, the word "employment" is a linguistic product of the capitalist era. A permanent level of unemployment presupposes a working population which is to a large extent dependent on a wage or salary for a living, without having other means of livelihood, as well as the right of enterprises to hire and fire employees in accordance with commercial or economic conditions.

5. As to the relationship between migration and the geoeconomics of capital (the geographic pattern of capital flow), Petras (2007) argues that *global flows of capital determine the direction of migration flows*. This

implies that capital accumulation takes place in the migrant-receiving countries through these flows, much of which result from the exploitation of the migrant-sending countries. Thus, the capitalist accumulate wealth in the receiving countries and immigrants follow the money by migrating to those centres with a high level of capital accumulation. Conversely Canterbury argues that the reverse is often the case — that "the internal and global flows of immigration determine the direction and flows of capital and that these are a major source of capital accumulation from migration processes in the current period of neoliberal capitalism dominated by financial capital" (Cantebury 2012: xi).

6. Many Marxists see this differently, seeing the long-term empirical trend towards the concentration and centralization of capital as a fundamental law of capitalist development, not the result of financialization.

7. There is actually a major ongoing debate as to the scope of the economic power wielded by these corporations. Some see this power, and the capitalist class behind it, as hegemonic, having eclipsed the economic power of the nation-state, which has been seriously, if not fatally, weakened by the globalization process. Those who argue this see the MNCs as an agency of the "new imperialism" (the means by which countries on the periphery of the system are dominated). Contrary to this "world systems" perspective, most Marxists continue to argue that imperialism implies the projection of state power in support of capital — identifying the economic interests of capital at each stage of its development with the "national interest."

8. That the capitalist class, by virtue of its property in the means of production, commands the levers of economic power is not in dispute. What is very much disputed or unresolved, however, is how and to what degree this economic power translates into political power — whether or not the economically dominant capitalist class constitutes a ruling class.

References

Andreff, W. 2009. "Outsourcing in the New Strategy of Multinational Companies: Foreign Investment, International Subcontracting and Production Relocation." *Papeles de Europa* 18: 5–34.

Battelle. 2012. "2013 Global R&D Funding Forecast." Columbus, Ohio: Battelle. <http://www.rdmag.com/sites/rdmag.com/files/GFF2013Final2013_reduced.pdf>

Bello, Walden. 2005. *Dilemmas of Domination: The Unmaking of the American Empire*. New York: Metropolitan Books.

Canterbury, D. 2012. *Capital Accumulation and Migration*. Leiden: Brill.

Castro, Fidel. 2007. "The Brain Drain." *Cuban Agency News*, Havana, July 18. <http://www.voltairenet.org/article150116.html>.

Davis, Mike. 2006. *A Planet of Slums.* London: Verso.

Delgado Wise, Raúl, and James Cypher. 2007. "The Strategic Role of Mexican Labour Under NAFTA: Critical Perspectives on Current Economic Integration." *The Annals of the American Academy of Political and Social Science* 615: 120–42.

Delgado Wise, R., and H. Márquez. 2007. "The Reshaping of Mexican Labor Exports under NAFTA: Paradoxes and Challenges." *International Migration Review* 41(3).

Delgado Wise, R., H. Márquez and H. Rodríguez. 2004. "Organizaciones transnacionales de migrantes y desarrollo regional en Zacatecas." *Migraciones internacionales* 2, 4.

Denning, Michael. 2010. "Wageless Life." *New Left Review* 66: 79–97.

Duggan, Marie Christine. 2013. "Reserve Army of Labor and Migration." In E. Ness (ed.), *Encyclopedia of Global Human Migration.* Wiley Publishers.

Engels, Frederick. 1962 [1845]. "The Condition of the Working Class in England." In Karl Marx and Frederick Engels, *On Britain.* Moscow.

Foster, J.B., R.W. McChesney and J. Jonna. 2011a. "The Internationalization of Monopoly Capital." *Monthly Review* 63, 2: 3–18. <http://monthlyreview.org/2011/06/01/the-internationalization-of-monopoly-capital>.

____. 2011b. "The Global Reserve Army of Labour and the New Imperialism." *Monthly Review* 63, 6: 1–15.

Freeman, R.B. 2006. *The Great Doubling: The Challenge of the New Global Labor Market.* <http://emlab.berkeley.edu/users/ webfac /eichengreen/e183_sp07/great_doub.pdf>.

Frobel, F., J. Heinrichs and O. Kreye. 1980. *The New International Division of Labour: Structural Unemployment in Industrialised Countries and Industrialisation in Developing Countries.* Cambridge: Cambridge University Press.

Ghose, Ajit K., Nomaan Maji and Christoph Ernst. 2008. *The Global Employment Challenge.* Geneva: ILO (International Labour Organisation).

ILO (International Labour Organization). 2011. *Global Employment Trends 2011: The Challenge of a Jobs Recovery.* Geneva: International Labour Organisation.

Márquez, Humberto, and Raúl Delgado Wise. 2011. "Signos vitales del capitalismo neoliberal: Imperialismo, crisis y transformación social." *Estudios Críticos del Desarrollo* I, 1 (junio–diciembre): 11–50.

Marx, Karl. 1969 [1898]. *Value, Price and Profit.* New York: International Co. <http://www.marxists.org/archive/marx/works/download/pdf/value-price-profit.pdf>.

____. 1954 [1867]. *Capital: A Critique of Political Economy,* Vol. 1. Moscow: Progress Publishers. <http://www.marxists.org/ archive/marx/works/download/pdf/Capital-Volume-I.pdf>.

____. 1847. *Wages*. December.

McKinsey Global Institute. 2012. *The World at Work: Jobs, Pay, and Skills for 3.5 billion People*. McKinsey & Co. <http:// www.mckinsey.com/insights/ employment_and_growth/the_world_at_work>.

Moseley, F. 1995. "Capital in General and Marx's Logical Method: A Response to Heinrich's Critique." *Capital & Class* 56: 15–48.

OECD (Organisation for Economic Co-operation and Development). 2008. *Open Innovation in Global Networks*. Copenhagen: OECD. <http://www. oecd.org/sti/openinnovationinglobalnetworks.htm>.

Petras, James. 2007. "Mesoamerica Comes to North America: The Dialectics of the Migrant Workers' Movement." Retrieved January 6, 2009 from <http://petras.lahaine.org/articulo.php?p=6&more=1&c=1>.

Petras, James, and Henry Veltmeyer. 2013. *Social Movements in Latin America*. Basingstoke, UK: Palgrave Macmillan.

Pochmann, Marcio, et al. 2004. *Atlas da exclusâo no mundo*, 5 vols. Sao Paulo: Cortez Editora.

RIMD (Red Internacional de Migración y Desarrollo). 2015. *La migracion calificada en y desde america del sur*. Unidad Estudios del Desarrollo, Universidad Autónoma de Zacatecas.

Roldán, Genoveva (ed.). 2013. *La globalización del subdesarrollo en el mundo del trabajo*. Mexico: UNAM-Instituto de Investigaciones Económicas.

Sassen, Saskia. 1988. *The Mobility of Labour and Capital: A Study in International Investment and Labour Flow*. Cambridge University.

Sturgeon, Timothy. 2003. "What Really Goes On in Silicon Valley? Spatial Clustering and Dispersal in Modular Production Networks." *Journal of Economic Geography* 3, 2: 199–225.

World Bank. 2011. *Migration and Remittances Factbook 2011*. <http://siteresources.worldbank.org>.

Chapter 5

The Social Dimension of Migration, or the Underside of Development

The capitalist development of the forces of production, or "economic development" in the jargon of development discourse, has not been without costs — economic, social and environmental. Indeed, these costs — the underside of the enormous progress that has been made in expanding the forces of production on a global scale — are staggering, even without a full accounting of them. One of these costs is social: the dependence on work or labour that has negative consequences for workers' health and well-being, including a trampling on their rights to organize in the struggle to protect and advance their interests. The Mexican government, for example — and the same applies to export-processing or "free trade" zones in other parts of the global south — have guaranteed capital (owners and investors) that the *maquiladora* assembly plants will be union free. One effect of this policy is a reduced capacity of workers to negotiate higher wage rates and improved conditions, a situation that is reflected in the reduction of wages that has hit workers in the *maquiladora* sector in recent years, presumably in response to competitive pressures from Chinese exports. Bendensky (2005) reported that wages in this sector in 2005 were on average 24 percent lower than real wages earned in December 2000. Moreover, real wages for Mexican manufacturing workers in 2000 were only 72.5 percent of their 1982 level, according to Unger's data in 2002.

Another social cost of capitalist development and globalization is a dependence of jobs on an industry owned by foreigners, making both workers and the economy vulnerable to the vicissitudes of global capital. Evidence of this vulnerability is the growing trend to relocate *maquiladoras* to countries, such as China, with even cheaper sources of labour. A race to the bottom, one might argue. Whereas workers in Mexico receive around 20 percent of national income in the form of wages (versus 30–40 percent in many European countries), Chinese workers, it is estimated, receive only 6 percent of the national income, allowing the Chinese government to orchestrate one of the highest savings and investment rates in the world (40 percent), a major factor in China's incredible record of rapid economic growth over ten years of 10 percent annual growth, four times greater than the rate ever experienced by the industrialized countries such as the U.S. in their history, and twice the rate of annual growth experienced by many countries prior to the neoliberal era, in the period of what historians have dubbed "the golden age of capitalism" (1948–1970).

Rural Emigration:
Economic Opportunity or a World of Slums?

In the 1990s, within the institutional and policy framework of the post-Washington consensus as to the need for a more inclusive form of capitalist development, the working class confronted a major campaign by organizations such as the World Bank for labour market reform. The aim of this campaign was to create political conditions for a new and more flexible regime of capital accumulation and mode of labour regulation: to give capital, in its management function, more freedom to hire, fire and use labour as needed; and to render labour more flexible, that is, disposed to accept wages offered under free market conditions and to submit to the new management model of its relation to capital and the organization of production. As the World Bank at the time saw it, widespread government interference in the labour market and workplace (e.g., minimum wage legislation), as well as excessive (monopoly) union power, distorted the workings of the free market, leading capital (investors) to withdraw from the production process, thereby generating problems of unemployment, poverty and informality.

To address these "problems," labour legislation protecting employment has been replaced by laws that enhance the arbitrary power of employers to fire workers, reduce compensation for firings and hire temporary and casual labour. Such deregulation of the labour and other markets has led to new rules that facilitate new investments and the transfer of profits, but also result in massive decimation of stable jobs for workers, increased marginality for and within many communities, and sharply polarized national economies.

Disparities in wealth and access to productive resources are reflected in a concentration of income within the capitalist class and the spawning of a number of enormously rich capitalists, mostly rentiers and very large investors but also corporate executives — *Fortune*'s super rich billionaires (Milanovic 2012). Studies have established that the world's wealth is now divided into two: almost half going to the richest 1 percent; the other half to the remaining 99 percent (Oxfam 2014: 1). The wealth of the richest 1 percent world amounts to US$110 trillion, which is sixty-five times the total wealth of the bottom half. In fact, Oxfam estimates that by 2016 the total wealth of the richest 1 percent will be equivalent to the total wealth of the other 99 percent (5). And only a tiny fraction of this small group (around 0.00001 percent of the world population) is found in Forbes' list of 1,426 individuals, almost exclusively a men's club, with a combined net worth of $5.4 trillion (Kroll 2013). Just eighty-five members of this exclusive club of super rich capitalists dispose of the same amount of wealth as owned by the bottom half of the world's population. Mexico's Carlos Slim, owner of large monopolies in Mexico and elsewhere, could pay the yearly wages of 440,000 Mexicans with income derived from his wealth (Milanovic 2012: 9).[1]

The poorest households dispose of a reduced share of income that is growing little or not at all in real terms. One result is the generation of new forms and conditions of poverty and social exclusion that have even reached well into the middle classes. A striking characteristic of imperial-induced inequality is the growth of the urban poor and the changing class composition of the poor: the new poverty is urban rather than rural and extends well beyond the working and producing classes into the once proud but now decimated middle class. While rural poverty continues to be the rule, the fastest growing number of poor today is found in the cities. The new urban poor are not simply "rural migrants" but include socially excluded and downwardly mobile workers and the lower-middle-class individuals who have been fired from their jobs and have found employment in the burgeoning informal sector. The growing armies of urban poor in Latin America now constitute a second and third generation of workers, many of whom live in slums or shantytowns, unable to follow the earlier generations' occupational ladder towards incremental improvement. One consequence of this class situation has been the skyrocketing growth of crime directly linked to family disintegration and concentrated among young people who earlier would have channelled their grievances through trade unions or the factory system.

Pillars of Social Exclusion

It has become fashionable to write of the urban poor as "socially excluded" rather than as poor. Not only is this new language more acceptable to the poor, who do not like to see themselves as such, but it is more convenient for the development agencies that have sprung up all over the urban landscape. The reason is that the term "socially excluded" draws attention away from relations of capitalist exploitation and oppression that are associated with more organized forms of class action. The conditions of social exclusion, which certainly includes low income and poverty, seem more amenable to redress and less violent political responses than does economic exploitation. A probable reason for this is that it is politically more feasible to design socially inclusive strategies of poverty reduction than to directly challenge the existing highly concentrated structure of economic power.

In fact, it is possible to conceive of the poor as both economically exploited and socially excluded. The social conditions of exploitation derive from the capital-labour relation, which, despite the transformative change in associated conditions of work — the growth of the so-called "informal sector" over the 1980s and 1990s — still defines the class situation of many if not most urban dwellers. First, urban workers in the so-called "informal sector" of economically marginal enterprises (street work "on one's own account" — to use the language of statisticians) are by no means disconnected from the capitalist system. In effect, they, like the unemployed and rural-to-urban migrants more generally, constitute an enormous reservoir of surplus labour for capital — what Marx in a different historic context termed an "industrial reserve army." This reserve army helps keep down the wages of workers in the formal sector of capitalist enterprise and foreign investment, and also serves to weaken labour in its capacity to organize and negotiate collective agreements.

Regarding social exclusion, the following six major "pillars," or structural conditions,[2] have been identified by development scholars (Paugam 1996; Pochmann 2004; Rojas 2013):

1. dispossession of the means of social production, reflected in the widespread conditions of landlessness, near-landlessness and rural outmigration;
2. lack of access to urban and rural labour markets and opportunities for wage employment, reflected in the low rate of labour force participation and the high rate of unemployment in the rural sector;
3. lack of access to "good quality or decent jobs," reflected most clearly in evidence of increased rates of super- and under-employment, and in the growth and prevalence of jobs that are contingent in form (seasonal, involuntary part-time, short-term, etc.) with a high degree of informality and inordinately low wages and other forms of remuneration;
4. reduced access to government social services in areas of social development, such as education, health and social security;
5. lack of access to stable forms of adequate income, reflected in the incapacity of many households to meet their basic needs and indicators of relative and absolute poverty[3]; and, above all,
6. exclusion from the apparatus of decision-making or "political power," reflected in the centralized nature of this power structure, elite control of this structure, the prevalence of client-patron relations in the political arena and frequent recourse to political organization and action in the form of anti-systemic social movements.

A New Dualism

Presidents Carlos Menem, Fernando Cardoso, Ernesto Zedillo and Eduardo Frei, in the heady years of the neoliberal policy agenda (the 1990s), all announced the entrance of their respective countries (Argentina, Brazil, Mexico, Chile) into the First World. They showcased modern shopping malls, the boom in cellular phones, supermarkets loaded with imported foods, streets choked with cars and stock markets that attracted big overseas speculators. Today, 15–20 percent of Latin Americans share a "First World" lifestyle: they send their kids to private schools; belong to private country clubs where they swim, play tennis and do aerobic exercises; get facelifts at private clinics; travel in luxury cars on private toll roads; and communicate via computer, fax and private courier service. They live in gated communities protected by private police. They frequently vacation and shop in New York, Miami, London and Paris. Their children attend overseas universities. They enjoy easy access to influential politicians, media moguls, celebrities and business consultants. They are usually fluent in English and have most of their savings in overseas accounts or in dollar-denominated local paper. They form part of the international circuit of the new imperial system. They are the audience to which presidents address their grandiloquent First World discourse of a new wave of global prosperity based on an adjustment to the requirements of the new world economic order. Despite the ups and downs of the economy they benefit from the imperial system.

But the rest of the population, mostly the social product of a rural-to-urban migration process, lives in an entirely different world. Cuts in social spending and the elimination of basic food subsidies have pushed peasants towards malnutrition and hunger. Large-scale redundancy of factory workers and their entry into the "informal sector" means a subsistence existence and dependence on the "extended family," community-based charities and "solidarity for survival," including soup kitchen and family remittances. Slashed public health and education budgets result in increasing payments and deteriorating services. Cuts in funds for maintenance of water, sewage and other public services have resulted in a resurgence of infectious diseases. Declining living standards measured in income and living conditions is the reality for two-thirds or more of the population. There has been a decline from Third World welfarism to Fourth World immiseration.

Child Migration: A Humanitarian Crisis (Mexico)

In the summer months of 2014 the news media in Mexico picked up on a problem that was by no means new but that had begun to hit crisis proportions — a humanitarian crisis constituted by the large number of unaccompanied child migrants on the road north to connect with family members. In just nine months American authorities deported over 50,000 unaccompanied children back to Mexico or their home country in Central America. Needless to say, this was but a small part of the problem, although it is difficult to determine the proportion of the successful cross-border migrants within this highly vulnerable segment of the migratory flows. What is evident is an increased vigilance by U.S. border guards and migration authorities in apprehending and then deporting unaccompanied children. In just one month (from April to May 2014), the number of unaccompanied underage migrants presented by the U.S. authorities to their Mexican counterparts went up by more than 260 percent. Over the year the increase was 709 percent.

There are no hard statistics on the phenomenon of unaccompanied children, but an analysis of a group of migrants from Guatemala and elsewhere in Central America that were apprehended by Mexican authorities in 2014 provides a glimpse into the scale of the problem. Of this group 35,858 were adults, i.e., 18 years old and over, while 8,007, or around 25 percent, were minors. Of this group of minors, 5,175 fell into the 12–17 age category (3,794 boys, 1,381 girls). In the youngest age bracket (0–11 years of age), 705 of the 2,832 migrants travelled unaccompanied. As for motivation, it seems that 80 percent sought to migrate to the U.S. with the intention of being reunited with family members, while 20 percent did so in hopes for a better life.

A number of studies have documented the problems experienced by these child migrants: many are victims of crimes involving personal violence, including assault and harassment, sexual abuse and robbery; many suffered from hunger and disease; and many others are trafficked for sex or virtual slave labour. These problems, as pointed out by Olga Sánchez Martínez (2013), director of an NGO support group and a recipient of Human Rights Award in 2004, have always existed, but the extreme violence associated with the drug trade tend to hide them from view.

Many of these documented problems are experienced by unaccompanied child migrants en route to the U.S. border, where there are no end of jackals and other individuals all ready to take advantage of and victimize this most vulnerable segment of the stream of illegal migrants across the border — abusing, trafficking or prostituting them. And other problems arise once the children manage to cross the border by themselves, or, as in many cases, in small groups formed en route or at the crossing. These problems include death from dehydration in the desert. Just in one state, Arizona, according to a newspaper report (*La Jornada*, December 28, 2014), the remains of 2,200 persons, many of them children, have been recovered since 2001.

Again, there are no reliable statistics on this, but it is likely that a greater percentage of unaccompanied children than adults make it into the U.S. or manage to reunite with family members. Of those unaccompanied child migrants that avoid death, many are rounded up by the U.S. border police and detained for eventual deportation. From October 2013 to June 2014, U.S. border police apprehended more than 52,000 unaccompanied children who entered the U.S. illegally, i.e., without the necessary documents. In the same period, some 53,000 unaccompanied children, many of them from Guatemala and other countries in Central America, were deported back to Mexico, their route of entry to the U.S. In just fifteen months 3,000 underage Mexican girls, 63 percent of them unaccompanied, were deported (*La Jornada*, July 3, 2014). Of the underage migrants who were accompanied by an adult family member, the vast majority were returned to their place of origin. As for the unaccompanied minors, two-thirds of them were detained indefinitely, presumably because of the difficulty of not knowing where to return them or having no one to turn them over to. According to José Jacques y Medina, an activist with the Movimiento Migrante Mesoamericano, U.S. authorities in 2013 deported 845 minors from Central America across the border from San Diego; but in the first five months of 2014 the number of child deportees aged 12 to 17 expelled had already reached 1,173. And there have been other reports of a stepped-up campaign to deport minors as well as adult undocumented migrants from Mexico and Central America.

This phenomenon is just the "tip of the iceberg" of a broader problem whose root causes have been underestimated. These are associated with the profound social inequalities along the Central America–Mexico–U.S. migration corridor and the increasing presence of organized crime along the migration journey.

Migration and Those Left Behind:
The Social Costs of Economic Development

> Walking amongst the tall buildings in a modern city of China will remind us of the countless rural labourers who perform the back-breaking work that supports urban construction and economic growth. As the migrant workers move from their villages, in search of better lives in the urban centres, they create another segment — the "left-behind" people — of China's population. The "left-behind" people are the family members of migrant workers who remain in their communities to perform farm labour and to look after their homes and remaining family members. Make no mistake about it, these "left-behind" people live tough lives.   —*Ye Jingzhong (2011: 613)*

A lot of the migration literature focuses on the problems and social condition of migrants at the destination points of the migration process. Other studies focus on the transnational relations that migrants themselves establish between their communities of origin and destination and the political economy of development — the dynamics and macro-economic development implications for sending and receiving societies in this process. Yet other studies concern the social conflicts and class struggles generated in the capitalist development of agriculture and associated forces of change. However, relatively few studies look at the problems of those left behind in the process of rural outmigration to the cities or abroad. But China is an exception in this regard. At the China Agricultural University a group of researchers, mostly sociologists, turned their research efforts to the problems created for the communities that are abandoned in the process of capitalist development and agrarian transformation (Jingzhong 2011; Jingzhong et al. 2013). The problem, as documented in the case of rural China, which has seen one of the most rapid, large-scale and far-reaching processes of social transformation and outmigration in both recent and recorded history, is that the bulk of the rural emigrants are adult males and other productive segments of the rural population, depriving the abandoned rural communities of their most productive human resource.

Figure 5.1 provides some idea as to the enormous scale of rural-to-urban migration in China over the past two decades, a process of productive and social transformation activated by an unprecedented growth in the total output of industries in the manufacturing sector, with a growth rate averaging 10 percent a year for almost three decades. As in Latin America, under different conditions but in the same conjuncture of global capitalist development, the movement en masse of workers from rural China to the cities started in the 1980s, along with the initiation of economic reform and the relaxation of the household registration (*hukou*) system. According to statistics based on a 1 percent population sample in 2005, the temporary worker population nationwide amounted to 147 million, or 2.05 percent more than in 2000 (Lin 2012). With accelerated urbanization, Ye Jingzhong adds, this trend will continue. Indeed, he notes that the National Demographic Development Strategy Report, issued in 2007, predicted that 300 million more rural people will move to cities and towns in the next twenty years. According to estimates

Figure 5.1 Labour Migration (1990s)

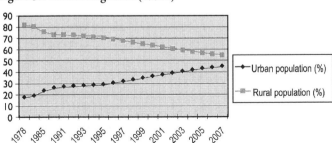

Source: Jingzhong 2014

made by the National Population and Family Planning Commission in 2009, there will be 500 million inhabitants in cities, 500 million in the countryside and 500 million floating between rural and urban over the next thirty years (Jingzhong 2011: 614).

Although the economic development of industrialized countries was in most cases accompanied by a continuous transfer of economic activity and people from rural to urban areas, regarded by development economists as unavoidable and necessary condition of economic development, Jingzhong notes that the movement of rural labourers to cities in China is distinctly different from what has happened and is happening in many countries in the global south. Generally speaking, he notes, the number of temporary urban workers in China is high, but the number of permanent "migrants" is actually quite low. That is, very few of the workers coming to the cities for work can or do become permanent urban residents. For most, urban areas are merely workplaces, not homes. Temporary migrants flow to and from the urban and rural areas seasonally and are often compared to migratory birds (Li 2009).

In the Latin American literature, such workers are called *golodrino* (swallows), in reference to landless and homeless workers, including women and children, who are involved in temporary agricultural activities in repetitive harvest cycles and subjected to highly exploitative working conditions. The situation in China is similar yet differs from the case of many rural landless workers in Latin America, who we have categorized as a semiproletariat, who float and move to the urban areas for work during the week but return to the rural communities in the countryside on weekends. This is particularly the case in countries such as Bolivia and Ecuador, with a high concentration of indigenous communities, and where a high rate of out-of-country migration is balanced with a high rate of a regular and constant (rather than seasonal) flow and movement from the rural communities to the urban and peri-urban centres. In China this semiproletariat takes a different form, that of "peasant workers" who work off-farm seasonally or migrate to the cities for waged work but return to their rural communities annually for the Chinese new year festival season (Meng 2011; Lin 2012).

An important feature of the large-scale seasonal or annual

migration to the cities is the social composition of the "left behind" population. CAU researchers have broken down this population into 58 million children, 47 million wives and 45 million elderly (Li 2009; Cai 2011; Jingzhong et al. 2013: 1119). Not only do the rural communities that are abandoned in the massive internal rural-urban migration process suffer the consequences of losing many productive members, but the women, elders and children are left to bear what is clearly a heavy social price of China's development process of rapid growth and urban-centred industrialization. This can be seen as the underside of China's economic boom.

The CAU research team headed by Jingzhong has documented at length and in great detail the heavy costs borne by the left behind population.[4] They include a split family life. Although reunited at the Chinese New Year — the spring festival — most families are split on average for ten years (Jingzhong 2011: 615). "Parental affection and guidance," Jingzhong notes, "are of vital importance for children in their childhood and adolescence," yet, due to the migration of their parents, he adds "these supports are absent in the life of the left-behind children" (ibid.). It is estimated that in 2009 there were at least 50 million Chinese children in this situation (ibid.).

CAU researchers documented the following other negative impacts of parental migration and split families: (1) the emotional needs of most left behind children are neglected; (2) left behind girls are often burdened by heavy labour and psychological pressures and are generally more vulnerable compared to left behind boys; (3) migrant parents do not play the necessary roles in the psychological development of left behind children, over-emphasizing material compensation and underestimating intimate care; (4) the ethics, norms and value systems of left behind children, and thus their behaviour, tend to be overly influenced by and biased towards an increasingly dominant modern culture and lifestyle; and (5) lacking parental support, the education of left behind children is comparatively more limited than the education of children in households where parents have not migrated, thus reducing the children's horizons and opportunities (Jingzhong 2011).[5]

At a more general level the findings of CAU researchers also confirm the theory and macro-level arguments advanced by the advocates of a political economy approach to understanding the dynamics of migration and development, namely that these dynamics engage systemic forces that operate beyond the limits and management capacity of public policy and institutional reform. For example, after devoting "their golden youth" to the cities, mostly for the better education and life options of their next generation — generating wealth by providing cheap labour and productive human capital — migrants generally return to the countryside, where the rural communities and their families have to take care of them for the rest of their lives. When their offspring grow up they tend to follow the same routine as their parents, i.e., work in the cities and return to the countryside when they get old, so maintaining a system of labour reproduction at no cost to the capitalist class, which has accumulated vast pools of capital and enriched themselves at the expense of the urban proletariat and the rural communities. Thus, the rural areas continue to provide the cities — more precisely the urban-based capitalist class — with cheap surplus labour and productive human capital, and assume the reproduction costs of capital (the human and other costs of reproducing the labour force). And this is without considering the environmental dimension of capitalist development, in China and elsewhere on the periphery of the world capitalist system, namely the provision by the countryside of raw materials and natural resources, such as minerals and metals to fuel the accumulation process and industrial development in the cities, leaving "many places in the countryside destroyed with open holes and barren mountains" (Jingzhong 2011: 619). The conclusion drawn by Jingzhong from these findings in the case of China is that "the rural has continuously infused nutrients and life blood [not to mention 'cheap surplus labour'] to the cities, and have left their own veins open" in the process.

The Resistance to Capitalist Development: The Class Struggle for Land and Everyday Forms of Resistance

Migration has been a dominant demographic response to the forces of capitalist development and social change — powerful forces that included industrialization and urbanization and, as of the 1980s, neoliberal globalization. By the end of the Second World War, which initiated another phase in the capitalist development of the forces of production, the dynamic forces released in the development process had brought about a significant demographic shift of the population from the rural areas to the expanding capitalist nucleus in the urban centres of a society in transition. On the periphery of the system, however, production was still predominantly organized around agriculture, and society was predominantly rural. But in the wake of the Second World War, the capital accumulation process was reactivated, giving rise to a new dynamic of social change on the periphery.

This dynamic can be traced out in cycles, each characterized by a different response to the forces of change and development liberated or generated in the process. One was for the proletarianized and impoverished peasant farmers — the peasantry, as we understand them and they identify themselves — to adjust to these forces by abandoning their rural communities and migrating to the cities and smaller urban centres. The other response was to resist these forces and struggle to retain their connection to the land. In the context of the 1950s and 1960s in Latin America, this response led to the formation and spread of social movements by landless rural workers organized for the purpose of achieving national liberation (from U.S. imperialism) and revolutionary social change.[6] A notable outcome of this struggle was the Cuban Revolution in 1959. The nation-states and international organizations that had come together to advance the capital accumulation process responded to this resistance in two ways: first, by deploying the state apparatus of armed force and launching military operations against the revolutionary movements; second, by opening up another front in the class war and launching a project of integrated rural development, designed to pacify the revolutionary ferment in the countywide by giving the "rural poor" an alternative to the confrontational approach of the revolutionary social movements. By the end of the 1970s, under the onslaught of these two offensives, all but one of the armies of national liberation were defeated or brought to ground.

In the 1980s, by deploying their power to force governments in the region to change course, the agents of the U.S. imperial state created conditions that would lead to a fundamental realignment of macroeconomic policy of these governments with the Washington consensus regarding the virtues of free market capitalism. The immediate response to this "development" in the popular sector was resistance to the neoliberal policy agenda, implemented under the dictates of this consensus.

In the 1980s this resistance predominantly took the form of spontaneous protests by the urban masses of recent rural migrants against the "IMF reforms" implemented by governments. By the 1990s, however, the resistance against the structural reform agenda of these neoliberal regimes had become more organized in the form of new sociopolitical movements with their social base in rural landless workers, organizations of peasant producers and the indigenous social movements (Petras and Veltmeyer 2001, 2013).

As in the 1950s and 1970s, governments in the region that were aligned with the neoliberal policy agenda responded to the popular movements by enlisting the cooperation of the international organizations engaged in the "development" project and the participation of the civil society organizations, or nongovernmental organizations, that had formed in the vacuum left by the state in its retreat from a dominant role in the economy. In the context of a new (post-Washington) consensus, as to the need to bring the state back into the development process and secure a more sustainable and more socially inclusive form of development, the architects of the international development project changed course. Departing from a strategy of encouraging the "rural poor" to migrate in the search for greener pastures and greater "economic opportunity" in the modern labour markets, the officials of the international organizations and financial institutions such as the World Bank, which had assumed leadership in the fight against global poverty, turned towards a new strategy of encouraging the rural poor to remain in their communities — to engage in a process of community-based local development rather than emigration. The end result of this strategic shift was to turn many of the rural poor away from the social movements that had led the resistance against neoliberalism, weakening these movements in the process. Large numbers of the rural poor continued — and continue — to emigrate, impelled by forces that left, and leave, them very few options. But the momentum had begun to shift towards local development — allowing the dispossessed rural poor to stay and subsist in their communities by diversifying their sources of household income, with the additional support of remittances and direct money transfers to the poor by governments (Veltmeyer and Tetreault 2013).

Conclusion

Capitalist development of the forces of production over the course of the twentieth century and into the twenty-first has generated a process of social and productive transformation, which in turn has given rise to a range of popular responses to the forces of change released in this process. An analysis of these responses in diverse historical contexts and geographical locations on the periphery of the world capitalist system reveals two basic types of popular responses to the forces of change. One was *migration* — for the proletarianized small-landowning agricultural producers to take flight as it were, to abandon agriculture and take one or both of the development pathways out of rural poverty paved by the development agencies (labour, migration). The other response was *resistance* — to resist the forces of capitalist development and change and to mobilize in the form of social movements.

In the 1990s, a decade into the neoliberal era of capitalist development and the new world order, a third type of response in the popular sector of rural society had materialized. The response was to neither migrate in the search for employment (wage labour or self-employment) nor to join the social movements in the form of direct collective action, but for the rural landless workers, peasant and indigenous communities to seek a way to subsist by diversifying sources of household income. The solution, aided and abetted by the state in a strategic project of community-based local development, with international cooperation and social participation (engagement of civil society organizations), was pluriactivity: to combine agriculture, off-farm labour (the source of some 50 percent of household income) and income from remittances with micro-credit or micro-projects and reliance on cash transfers from the government, in designing an "exit path" out of rural poverty (De Janvry and Sadoulet 2000).

The new millennium, in a different conjuncture of capitalist development (extractive capitalism),[7] created an entirely new context for the development process — and for the inevitable resistance. This context included the demise of the neoliberal model, a tilt to the left in a political process of regime change, and a turn of these regimes towards a new development approach based on "inclusionary state activism." In addition, the growing demand for primary commodities (oil and gas, minerals and metals, agro-food products) led many governments in south America to turn towards extractivism (the extraction of natural resources, primary commodity exports) as a strategy of economic development, a strategy that led to the emergence of socioenvironmental and political movements by those directly affected by the operations of extractive capital, and new forms of resistance (Veltmeyer and Petras 2014).

Notes

1. What is even worse about these figures is that much of the income available to this class is undeclared. For example, revenues from narcotrafficking in Mexico, the proceeds of which are distributed among crony politicians, bankers and others and exceed revenues from Mexico's principal export (oil), are grossly under-reported.

2. In its 1992 report, IFAD (Jazairy 1992) identified up to twenty sources of rural poverty, including the structural sources or pillars identified below. As for the social conditions of this social exclusion and poverty, the associated literature, most of it generated in the past decade, is voluminous, as reflected in the ILO's 1994 compilation of studies. Given the array of international organizations and research institutions, both within the U.N. system and the international development community, involved in the war against poverty and the broader conditions of social exclusion, it is clear that the problem has not only reached critical proportions but that it is global in scope. One of many organizations set up in the search for solutions to the problem of social exclusion is the Research Centre for Analysis of Social Exclusion, established in October 1997 at the London School of Economics and Political Science with funding from the U.K. Economic and Social Research Council.

3. A poverty-oriented basic needs approach dominated the study of international development in the 1970s. Originating in the 1973 discovery of the World Bank that upwards of two-fifths of the world's population was in a state of relative deprivation, unable to meet its basic needs.

According to Amartya Sen, a household without sufficient income to meet the basic needs of its members is poor, a condition that can be measured in terms of a head count, that is, the number and percentage of the population that falls below a defined income poverty line; or, according to Sen, by an index of disparity in income distribution, viz., income gap ratio multiplied by the number of the poor, which provides a coefficient of specific poverty.

4. The study of the "left behind" population has been hampered by the lack of consensus as to definition. For example, should the upper age limit of left behind children be 16, 18 or even 21? How long should peasant workers migrate out before their children, spouses and parents can be counted among the left behind? Does it include the entire rural population left behind in the transition to capitalism? (Jingzhong et al. 2013: 1125).

5. The findings about the left behind population in China are comparable to those in other countries where those left behind in the transition to capitalism has been studied. On a review of these studies and their findings see Jingzhong et al. (2013). Some interesting regional and country variations have been found in regard to education, a most important development indicator. For example, in India a girl's chances of being educated are reported to be lower when fathers emigrate because they have to take on more domestic duties (Srivastava and Sasikumar 2003). Similar findings are recorded in China (Meyerhoefer and Chen 2011). However, Acosta (2011) reports that remittances in El Salvador result in a decrease of child labour and an increase in girls' schooling. In Mexico, it appears that a father's emigration leads to a reduction of expenditures on boys' education compared to girls, but if mothers migrate with their husbands it is more likely that they will invest in their children's education than when fathers migrate alone (Antman 2010; Jingzhong et al. 2013: 1126). Given these regional and country variations in findings it is evident that a lot more research is needed to determine the cause of these variations. Evidently the social dimension of migration is an exceedingly complex phenomenon that does not permit easy cross-country comparisons.

6. These social movements mobilized diverse forces of resistance and opposition to imperialist and class exploitation, including organized labour and the political left. However, the popular struggle was led by movements with their social base in the peasantry. For the dynamics of this struggle and these movements to reclaim the land see, inter alia, Veltmeyer (2008).

7. On the complex economic, social and political dynamics of this phase of capitalist development, see, inter alia, Veltmeyer and Petras (2014).

References

Acosta, P. 2011. "School Attendance, Child Labour and Remittances from International Migration in El Salvador," *Journal of Development Studies* 57, 6: 913–36.

Antman, F. 2010. "International Migration, Spousal Control and Gender Discrimination in the Allocation of Household Resources." Working Paper. Boulder Department of Economics.

Bendensky, León (2005), "La Inflación," *La Jornada*, 15 de agosto.

Cai, M. 2011. "Ministry of Civil Affairs Reported We Now Have 47 Million Left-Behind Wives." Xinhua News Agency. <http://news.qq.com/20110307/002362.htm>.

De Janvry, Alain, and Elisabeth Sadoulet. 2000. "Rural Poverty in Latin America: Determinants and Exit Paths." *Food Policy* 25: 389–409.

Jazairy, Idriss, Mohiuddin Alamgir and Theresa Panuccio. 1992. The State of World Rural Poverty. London: Intermediate Technology Publications (for IFAD).

Jingzhong, Ye. 2011. "Left-Behind Children: The Social Price of China's Economic Boom." *Journal of Peasant Studies* 38, 3 (July): 613–50.

Jingzhong, Ye, Chunyu Wang, Huifang Wu, Congzhi He and Juan Liu. 2013. "Internal Migration and Left-Behind Populations in China." *Journal of Peasant Studies* 40, 6: 1119–46.

Kroll, L. 2013. "Inside the 2013 Billionaires List: Facts and Figures." Forbes, 4 March. <http://www.forbes.com/sites/luisakroll/2013/03/04/inside-the-2013-billionaires list-factsand-figures>.

Li, F. 2009. "National Women's Federation Reported We Now Have 58 Million Left-Behind Children." Xinhua New Agency. <http://news.xinhuanet.com/societ/2009-05/26/content_11440077.htm>.

Lin, Jin. 2012. "Rights-Based Approach to the Educational Experience of Migrant Children in China." MA thesis, Institute of Social Studies, The Hague, The Netherlands, December.

Meng, Q. 2011. "Semi-Proletarianization, Commercialization of the Laborforce and Chinese Peasant-Workers." *Economics Study of Shanghai School* I: 135–53.

Meyerhoefer, C.D., and C.J. Chen. 2011. "The Effect of Parental Labor Migration on Children's Educational Progress in Rural China." *Review of Economics of the Household* 9, 3: 379–96. doi:10.1007/s11150-010-9105-2.

Milanovic, Branko. 2012. The Haves and the Have-Nots. New York: Basic Books.

Sánchez Martínez, M. Olga. 2013. "Los derechos de las mujeres <http://dialnet.unirioja.es/servlet/articulo?codigo=4229226>: un proceso inconcluso, clave de progreso." El derecho humano al desarrollo

<http://dialnet.unirioja.es/servlet/libro?codigo=516449>. Edited by por María Isabel Garrido Gómez <http://dialnet.unirioja.es/servlet/autor?codigo=297392>. Madrid: Editorial Tecnos.

Oxfam. 2014. "Working for the Few: Political Capture and Economic Inequality." Briefing Paper, January 20.

Paugam, Serge (ed.). 1996. *L' exclusion. L'Etat des savoirs.* Paris: Ed. La Découverte.

Petras, James, and Henry Veltmeyer. 2013. *Social Movements in Latin America.* Basingstoke UK: Palgrave Macmillan.

____. 2001. *Globalization Unmasked.* Halifax: Fernwood Publications.

Pochmann, Marcio, et al. 2004. *Atlas da exclusão no mundo,* 5 vols. Sao Paulo: Cortez Editora.

Rojas, Teresa. 2013. "Migración y exclusión social de los trabajadores del campo en México." *Revista Universitaria* 12. <http://www.educa.upn.mx/hecho-en-casa/num-11/152-migracion-y-exclusion-social-de-los-trabajadores-del-campo-en-mexico>.

Srivastava, R., and S. Sasikumar. 2003. "An Overview of Migration in India, Its Impacts and Key Issues." Country Overview Paper, Regional Conference on Migration, Development and Pro-Poor Policy Choices in Asia. Dhaka, Bangladesh: DFID.

Veltmeyer, Henry. 2008. "La dinámica de las ocupaciones de tierras en América Latina." In Sam Moyo and Paris Yeros (eds.), *Recuperando la tierra: El resurgimiento de movimientos rurales en África, Asia y América Latina.* Buenos Aires: CLACSO.

Veltmeyer, Henry, and James Petras. 2014. The New Extractivism. London: Zed Books.

Veltmeyer, Henry, and Darcy Tetreault. 2013. *Poverty and Development in Latin America Public Policies and Development Pathways.* Kumarian Press.

Chapter 6

Rethinking the Migration-Development Nexus

Led by the World Bank and the Inter-American Development Bank, some international organizations have been pursuing an international political agenda in the area of migration and development. They posit that remittances sent home by migrants can promote local, regional and national development in the countries of origin. By extension, remittances are seen as an indispensable source of foreign exchange that provides macroeconomic stability and alleviates income poverty. The evidence for this view is provided by a growing body of data on the importance of remittances as a source of income for many rural households in underdeveloped countries. The UNDP (2007) estimates that some 500 million people, or some 350 billion households, receive remittances. According to World Bank figures, remittances sent home by migrants from underdeveloped countries rose from US$85 billion in 2000 to US$435 billion in 2014. Taking into account unrecorded flows through informal channels, this figure could be 50 percent greater, which means that total remittances exceed total official foreign aid by a factor of two (World Bank 2014).

Although the World Bank's position regarding the relationship between remittances and migration has been cautious (Lapper 2006), the neoliberal policies of structural reform promoted by the World Bank and the IMF are the root cause of the upsurge in south-north migration and the flow of remittances over the past two decades. Moreover, as noted in this book, far from contributing to the development of migrant-sending countries, these policies have reinforced the dynamics of underdevelopment. The great paradox of the migration-development agenda is that it leaves neoliberal globalization intact and does not address the specific way in which neoliberal policies are applied in migrant-sending countries or the fundamental issues of development, such as (1) the negative impacts of migration on the migrants and their families — the human rights and human security concerns underlying contemporary migration — and, more importantly, (2) the root causes of forced migration, i.e., the urgent necessity to reduce the growing asymmetries that exist between sending and receiving countries and that are at the core of the capitalist trend towards uneven development.

This chapter seeks to cut through the complexities of the migration-development nexus and to highlight the need for an alternative approach based on the political economy of development. Special attention is placed on the role of migrant labour and remittances as part of a complex set of transnational social relations used for the subsistence of a surplus population that is forced to enter cross-border labour markets under conditions of social exclusion and below-subsistence wages. The chapter is organized into three parts. The first provides a brief overview of current theoretical models for analyzing the migration-development nexus. Next we identify six elements of a mythology that is widely used in the theoretical and political discourse on migration and development to obfuscate the workings of the world capitalist system in regard to the development process. Finally, we introduce an alternative model based on the political economy of development.

The Development-Migration Nexus: A Theoretical Overview

Despite a recent boom in migration and development research there is a clear dissociation between theories of development and theories of migration. This results in many studies that do not capture the fundamental dynamics of migration and the development process today. Also, as a result, theorization about the migration-development nexus lags behind and does not properly inform the migration discourse and development policies that are promoted by international organizations and widely adopted by policymakers.

The most influential migration studies have been undertaken by research centres in the developed countries, which, for obvious reasons are the major migrant-receiving countries on the planet. As we have observed, these have failed to pay enough attention to the workings of the world capitalist system, which underlies the migration process historically and today. At the moment there does not exist a theoretical-conceptual framework that takes into account the standpoint from which most scholars in the global south view the migration and development process, which is that the underdeveloped countries function as an enormous reserve army of surplus labour, that they are exporters of both cheap labour and highly skilled labour, and as such constitute a lever of capital accumulation on a global scale.

Most studies in the field of migration and development oddly enough tend to view the processes involved as separate, one having little to do with the other. The exception to this are those studies that treat migration as an independent variable (via remittances, the circulation of brain power, and the resources and initiatives, and transnational organizations, of migrants themselves) and development as the dependent variable in a chain of causation. As we have noted, an alternative approach, based on the political economy of capitalist development, connects both migration and development to the formation of a global labour market, the workings of the capitalist system in both developed and underdeveloped societies, and the role of central governments in controlling, regulating and managing the flow of migrants across national boundaries. However, both approaches have tended to converge in the analysis — and opposing views — on four critical issues: (1) the role and development implications of migrant remittances; (2) the diaspora and the formation of transnational organizations of migrants in the development process; (3) codevelopment; and (4) migrants as agents and an agency of local development.

1. *Remittances and productive investment.* During the last two decades of the twentieth century, the flow of Mexican workers to the U.S. increased notoriously with the implementation of neoliberal policies of "structural reform" under the Washington consensus and the integration of the two economies with NAFTA. Studies on migration and development in this context that focus on potential of remittances as a source of productive investment have been undertaken and advanced in two successive periods, giving rise to an ongoing debate and without providing theoretical or practical solutions to the problem.

In the 1980s, Reichert (1981), Stuart and Kearney (1981), Mines (1981) and Wiest (1984) undertook several empirical studies in the central-west region of Mexico to argue that migrant remittances had a negative effect in communities of origin, leading to social differentiation, land price inflation and the accumulation of local resources into the hands of a few. Subsequent studies in the 1990s, however, argued that the remittances did indeed have a productive role (Durand 1994; Jones 1995; Massey and Parrado 1998). The results of these studies indicated that remittances were invested in agricultural and human capital and that the circulation of money not only provided families with subsistence funds but, in the provision of investment funds, played a positive role in the development of local, municipal and regional economies. Some authors (Durand 1994; Jones 1995) argued that these investments had a substantial impact on specific sectors and localities, while others (Massey and Parrado 1998: 18) argued that international migration via collective remittances had a broader development impact as a "source of production capital" (the financing of productive investments and social infrastructure) and as a "dynamic force that promotes entrepreneurial activity, the founding of businesses and economic expansion" in high-migration areas where public and private investment are negligible (Goldring 1996; Smith 1998; Moctezuma 2000). Overall, the most interesting aspect of this research is the identification of a new social subject: the collective migrant (Moctezuma 1999), although the proponents of this concept — especially Moctezuma but also Torres (2000) and Ratha (2003), who respectively represent the institutional viewpoints of ECLAC and the World Bank — have been criticized, and rightly so, for painting an overly optimistic picture of the phenomenon (Binford 2002; Canales and Montiel 2004).

2. *Transnationalism and development.* Contrary to the assumption that migrants almost invariably cease contact with their place of origin once they have settled in their country of destination, transnationalism underscores quite the opposite: regardless of their incorporation into the receiving society, migrants tend to maintain strong ties with their society of origin. Authors who take this view argue that (1) migrants maintain bonds to their place of origin in order to deal with racial inequality and other hurdles in the

countries of destination; (2) migration is caused by global processes that supersede the nation-state and generates a global civil society that threatens the political monopoly exercised by the state and (3) transnationalism gives way to a "third space" that locates migrants between the sending and receiving states and their societies of origin and destination.

The link between transnationalism and development has been explored from at least two viewpoints. One is the economy of migration, where the transnational practices of migrants, such as phone calls, the use of communications technologies, participation in tourism and the nostalgia industry, and remittances have positive effects on local economies (Orozco 2003) but also create niches that are later appropriated by transnational corporations (Guarnizo 2003). The second viewpoint concerns the contribution of migrant organizations to local and regional development processes, particularly their participation in social works that collectively benefit local populations (Delgado Wise, Márquez and Rodríguez 2004; Portes, Escobar and Walton 2006).

3. *Codevelopment.* Some nations of the European Union (France and, more recently, Italy and Spain) have designed country-specific policies of codevelopment that are based on the migrants' potential development contributions to their place of origin with the support of the developed nations. Codevelopment seeks to (1) promote productive activities through remittances; (2) educate migrants and encourage their return to their place of origin; (3) involve migrants in cooperation projects; (4) educate and guide potential emigrants in the place of origin; (5) create bridges between communities of origin in the south and those who have emigrated to the north; (6) foster interaction between national governments, local civil and business organizations, universities, education and cultural centres and migrants, and (7) improve the living and working conditions of migrants. In practice, codevelopment has been used as a supra-governmental policy to control immigration flow, while less attention has been paid to the promotion of development in countries of migratory origin. The actors involved in the process of codevelopment (governments, migrant organizations and NGOs) do not necessarily see eye to eye on a number of issues, as their interpretations of

this concept usually adapt to their particular interests. Additionally, codevelopment is, in actuality, a paradox: less developed European Union countries such as Spain received Union support to increase their national development, to the extent that they went from being emigrant senders to immigrant receivers (Agrela and Dietz 2005). But when it comes to the outside and despite the ongoing demand for a cheap imported workforce, the European Union has created a sort of fortress (Bendel 2005) that seems to close its doors on immigration and uses codevelopment to cover up for immigration regulation policies involving countries that lie outside the Union rather than to actively pursue development in these nations.

4.   *Migrants as an agency of local development.* In the particular case of Mexico, Moctezuma (2005) has observed different types of migrants (collective, enterprising, savings-focused and retired) and the roles they play in terms of social and productive investments. Garcia Zamora (2003) has proposed the establishment of a fund for local development and the adoption of a microfinancing system,[1] while Delgado Wise and Rodríguez (2001) suggest that migrant organizations could promote regional development projects coupled with public policies.

From our perspective, the implementation of development alternatives demands the construction of a new collective social subject — one that involves migrant and non-migrant organizations — that can only have a limited impact in local and regional spaces within a capitalist context, which engenders uneven development and forced migration.

The Mythology of Migration and Development

Migration studies are fraught with underlying myths that distort reality under a decontextualized, reductionist and biased view of human mobility, particularly as regards labour migration. The dominant political and research agendas in the field tend to both use and reproduce this mythology, ignoring the context in which contemporary migration takes place as well as its root causes. That is, they assume that migration is a free and voluntary act and are oblivious to the structural forces released in the capitalist development process.

In addition, they tend to ignore the extraordinarily heavy costs of migration that are borne by both the migrant-sending countries and the migrants themselves. These costs, as we establish in Chapter 5, go well beyond the overemphasized positive impact of remittances.

The mythology underlying and reproduced in mainstream studies of migration and development can be deconstructed with regard to the following six basic myths:

MYTH 1: *North-South regional integration based on free-market principles leads to economic convergence and reduced migration.*
The great myth of global capitalism is the notion of the free market. In the drive to maximize profits individuals or companies flock to a supposedly common space — the market — where, free from state interference, they proffer goods that meet the needs and wants of consumers. Competition breeds innovation and favours companies that can offer products at lower prices via a process of innovation and technological conversion of production methods. Entrepreneurial freedom is a major force of production and encourages growth and prosperity.

On a regional level, free trade agreements provide for economic complementarity between countries with different mixes of productive resources and levels of development. Regional integration schemes based on the free circulation of tradeable goods and services, investment capital and labour — land allows for the extraction and mobilization of natural resources but, unlike capital and labour, is immobile — allows for a balance between production factors, allowing each country to take comparative advantage of their endowment of natural, manufactured and human resources for expanded production.

Mexico has faithfully followed the neoliberal precepts of the Washington consensus, but the purported success of its export model is an optical illusion in that what the country actually exports is its labour force, and the export model imposed on Mexico in the context of NAFTA has led to an asymmetrical integration of the country's economy with that of the United States (Cordera 2014). Table 6.1 provides a graphic representation of these asymmetries and their significant increase under NAFTA.

Table 6.1 Mexico-United States Asymmetries, 1994–2012

Asymmetries	Mexico		United States	
	1994	2012	1994	2012
Population (thousands)	93,055	115,640	259,753	308,827
GDP per capita (current U.S. dollars)	4,540	9,240	26,820	48,450
GDP (US$ billions at current prices/PPP)	717	1,747	7,031	15,011
Industrial production index	71.74	101.65	80.49	121.13
R&D spending (% GDP)	0.29	0.48	2.48	2.90
Population with university degree (% of the pop. 25–64)	11.90	18.30	27.98	38.50
Manufacturing wages (US$/hr.)	2.10	2.60	12.00	9.30
Unit costs of labour in manufacturing	95.20	90.40	96.30	98.60

Source: SIMDE. UAZ. Developed with data from INEGI, ENOE 4 trimestre 2012, and Banco de información económica, INEGI. U.S. Bureau of Labour Statistics BLS. Current Population Survey, 1994, 1995, 2011 and 2012.

Figure 6.1. Mexico–U.S. Migration 1840–2011

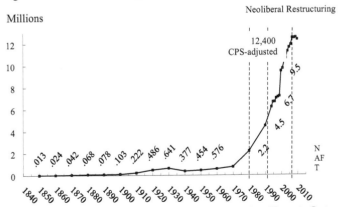

Source: Compiled from Decennial Censuses, 1850–1990; Pew Hispanic Center, 1994–2010 (Passel and Cohn 2014)

The promoters of NAFTA not only predicted a trend towards economic convergence but a decline in migration flows, which, as it turns out, have increased exponentially under NAFTA, with the appearance of an economic exodus (Figure 6.1).

MYTH 2: *Neoliberal restructuring promotes progress and social well-being.*
Economists in the mould of orthodox liberalism and neoclassical economics argue that the free market leads to general prosperity and mutual benefits, but what has in fact happened is that the vaunted structural adjustment programs, designed to liberate the "forces of economic freedom" from the regulatory constraints of the development state, resulted in a massive destruction on the periphery of the world capitalist system of major forces of production in both industry and agriculture. The production crisis brought about by this destruction forced millions of dispossessed and impoverished rural inhabitants to abandon their communities and migrate. The enormous exodus experienced by Mexico since the inception of NAFTA, a model of free trade, exposes the reality behind this myth.

MYTH 3: *Emigration under neoliberalism is a free and voluntary act.*
Conventional theories and discourses on migration present human mobility as a free act, a family or communal decision in search of economic opportunity, a way of building up resources that can be invested to improve quality of life and start a business. Migration dynamics are seen as organized by migrants themselves through social networks that also guide and channel them into the labour markets of the host economies. Migration flows and their organization acquire a life of their own to the point where they become their own cause, a cumulative movement that generates a culture of migration: a rite of passage for young people entering working and reproductive life, a sign of a people's identity.

This view of migration is little more than an apology, a form of false consciousness. The decision to migrate more often than not is a response to conditions over which migrants have no control and that they need to escape — destruction of the forces of production caused by the capitalist development of agriculture, dispossession of the means of production, poverty and unemployment and other labour market deficits.[2] Figure 6.2 it is revealing of the forces at play. It shows that from 2000 to 2010, Mexico's labour force increased by 9.6 million while formal jobs did so by a mere 2.1 million. This means a deficit of some 7.5 million jobs. The excluded workforce is distributed among the unemployed (1.5 million), informal workers (3.9 million) and migrants (2.1 million). It is striking that the volume of generated formal employment should be equal to the volume of migrants and that both categories added up (4.2 million) should be lower than the number of unemployed and informal workers (5.4 million). Coupled with previously outlined indicators of job insecurity, this highlights an important condition of forced outmigration in Mexico, a condition found in many underdeveloped and even developed countries (Roldán 2013).

MYTH 4: *Migration management through the balancing of the labour markets is beneficial for all stakeholders.*

Migration management is a key element of the dominant discourse underlying mainstream migration policies. These are promoted by multilateral agencies and think-tanks such as the International Organization for Migration (IOM), the Organization of American States (OAS) and the Migration Policy Institute (MPI). New nar-

Figure 6.2. Mexico: Labour Force Surplus or Job Deficit, 2000–2010

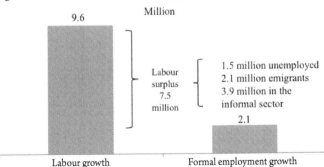

Sources: SIMDE, Mexico superavit. Estimates based on CPS, March Supplement, 2000 and 2010; and CEPALSTAT, Estadísticas de Empleo para América Latina, 2000–2010

ratives have been promoted through the umbrella of an apparently "neutral" notion associated with the all-embracing paradigm of "global governance" (Gosh 2007). These narratives attempt to depoliticize migration, obfuscate the existence of divergent interests or asymmetries and conflicts of power, avoid obligations imposed by international law and promote the idea that managing migration through the equilibrium of labour markets can be beneficial for all stakeholders: countries of destination, countries of origin and the migrants themselves. This unrealistic, triple-win scenario clearly favours the interests of the migrant-receiving countries and the large MNCs based in such countries.

MYTH 5: *Immigrants are a burden for receiving countries.*
It is usually thought that immigrant contributions to the host country are minimal and that, conversely, immigrant incorporation into the labour market constitutes an act of "generosity" that eventually leads to a decrease in economic productivity and loss of jobs for native workers. The truth, however, is very different, even though it has been concealed and distorted in public discourse and negatively influences public opinion. This topic has been left off bilateral and multilateral agendas, but more importantly it has been pushed aside as a result of the decision to address the issue unilaterally by treating border control as a matter of national sovereignty. Ultimately, this reflects the way in which the doctrine of national security, which tends to criminalize migrants, has become the benchmark for public migration policies.

MYTH 6: *Migrants are agents of development and their resources, mainly remittances, vehicles for development.*
Why such a surge of interest in the development implications and potential outcomes of migrant remittances, which are essentially wage earnings sent by workers to their financial dependents? As World Bank economist Devesh Kapur (2004) points out, remittances have become the new "development mantra" mainly because of the belief that they can serve as a mechanism of poverty reduction by adding to the income of poor households, or that they can be channelled into productive investments (on infrastructure, for

example) as a means of overcoming underdevelopment. Or, to put it less positively, the idea is that some of the most exploited and impoverished workers in the world can make up for the failure of mainstream development policies.

However, as argued by Canales (2011) and others, the economic impact attributed to remittances is totally disproportionate: the growth of the GDP through the multiplying effect of remittances is only 0.47 percent and the elasticity[3] of the GDP with regard to remittances is 0.036. As for the presumed impact of remittances on the poverty rate, according to Caneles it is in the order of 1.3 percentage points, the same as the impact of remittances in reducing inequality (re the Gini index). And the elasticity of poverty or inequality with regard to remittances is only 0.221.

Another promoted offshoot of the dominant discourse is "community development," which is ostensibly triggered by "collective remittances," in which migrant remittances are matched by the government in public works programs such as Mexico's "3 x 1" program. Even though it deploys very few fiscal resources (about 1 percent of total remittances), it is nevertheless portrayed as a source of community-based local development.

The fact is that remittances represent a fraction of the wages earned by migrant workers, most often in conditions of labour overexploitation, and aim to support financial dependents in the place of origin while contributing to family reproduction. This includes the formation of a workforce with a high propensity to migrate (e.g., children, siblings and other relatives) and support for the elderly and sick. Remittances play an essential role in ensuring social reproduction in conditions of poverty and social exclusion. The reality of overexploited migrant workers sending part of their wages to their poor dependents caught in a spiral of family and community degradation is far cry from the apologist discourse on migration.

Towards a New Model of the Migration-Development Nexus

Notwithstanding the current popularity of migration and development studies, the complexity of the subject requires an alternative approach that does not centre as much on the underlying motivation to migrate, and the consequences of this decision, as on the systemic dynamics involved as well as the macro-processes of development. From this political economy perspective, migration is viewed as one among other dimensions of the development process, as a field of structural dynamics and strategic practices that take place on global, regional, national and local levels. The theoretical and political approach taken by scholars and policymakers in the developed, migrant-receiving countries has created a hegemonic vision that must be countered by an approach that incorporates the viewpoints of the underdeveloped, migrant-sending countries — what we term the "perspective of the south." It is also important to promote a comparative analysis that examines the interactions between processes of migration and development and the particular experiences taking place within them in different places of the world in the context of global capitalism.

We are of the opinion that the problem of international migration should be systematically incorporated into the field of development studies and that processes of underdevelopment/development should be seen as a source of international migration (see Figure 6.3). In a context of large migration flows, the problem of development involves additional challenges, such as the asymmetric relations between countries, the reconfiguration of productive chains and the concomitant restructuring and precarization of the labour markets, trans-territorial social inequalities and, more specifically, the decline of the material and subjective foundations that propitiates a given population's emigration, along with issues involving their integration into receiving societies and their preservation of transnational ties.

From a theoretical standpoint, the fundamental challenge for researchers seeking to further examine these issues is the lack of an appropriate model that provides a theoretically simplified representation of the migration-development nexus, one that identifies the key variables and allows for both scientific analysis and theory construction. With reference to our findings and considerations regarding the migration-development nexus, such a model should include the following propositions:

- Migration studies should take into account the conditions and forces that are released or generated in the capitalist develop-

Figure 6.3 An Alternative Approach
to the Migration-Development Interrelation

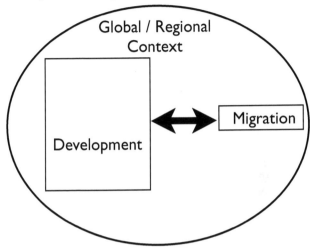

ment process (destruction of forces of production in agriculture, urbanization and modernization, globalization) as well as the strategic response to these forces, namely, to abandon agriculture and migrate in the search of a more viable livelihood, or to stay and fight — to resist rather than adapt to these forces.

• The process of capitalist development in the current conjuncture of neoliberal globalization entails the formation of a global reserve army of surplus labour and a massive outflow of migrant workers in a south-north direction, i.e., along the major faultline of the world capitalist system.

• The deepening of uneven development fostered by neoliberal globalization underdevelopment is a catalyst for a process of forced migration to developed countries, as well as a class struggle.

• Migrants make a significant contribution to economic development in the migrant-receiving country, which, in the neoliberal conjuncture of capitalist development, is predominantly, and increasingly, found in the global north at the centre of the system.

- Immigrants contribute to an overall lowering of the labour costs of production for capital, not only in the context of their existence and function as a global reserve of cheap and flexible labour, and a systemic tendency towards crisis and structural unemployment, but because they tend to be employed in labour-intensive areas of production where they substitute for a national workforce with higher wages and more benefits. This trend also increasingly relates to highly skilled migrants.

- International migration is the result of problems in the development process, and the migratory phenomenon has to be examined in this context in order reveal its root causes and effects. In order to study migration, its cause-and-effect interrelation with development, and examine the different stages inherent to this interaction, we must take into account two fundamental dimensions of the migration-development problematic: strategic practices and structural dynamics.

- Migrants help maintain precarious socioeconomic stability in their countries of origin. Wage-based remittances contribute to the subsistence of family members in the country of origin and to a lesser extent they also help finance small businesses in a subsistence economy.

- Studies of international migration should examine the development challenges faced by the migrant-sending countries as well as the economic and social costs of labour migration.

- Any study into the development-migration dynamic of the south-north relation — migration as a response to the dynamic forces of capitalist development — should analyze conditions that are specific to each region and country as well as generic to the operating capitalist system.

- Analysis of the migration-development nexus should include the dimension of space (local, national, regional and global) and time (the particular conjuncture of capitalist development), as well as the social dimension of the migration process (who benefits and who bears the costs?).

- The promotion of development as social transformation could contain the process of forced migration. Globalization depicts migration as inevitable, but we should endorse the viability of alternative processes of development, including resistance rather than adaptation to the forces of social change.

Conclusion

The theoretical framework proposed in this chapter concerns three issues that are fundamental for understanding the migration-development nexus:

The need for a critical approach to neoliberal globalization. In contrast to the dominant neoliberal discourse predicated on the virtues of free market capitalism and the inevitability of globalization (There Is No Alternative, as Margaret Thatcher famously declared), we posit that — given the contradictory features of capitalism — the current phase of capitalism is unsustainable and illegitimate, and that the neoliberal world order is *not* the end of history; on the contrary, capitalism at each phase of its development generates forces of resistance and a class struggle in one form or the other. Whether the correlation of forces in the class struggle will bring about the demise of the system is debateable. But what is clear enough is that the forces of change that are generated in the development process can be mobilized either to the left (in the interest of social equity and justice) or to the right (in the interest of capital accumulation). Social change is thus on the horizon.

A reconstitution of the field of development studies. The mode of analysis based on the belief that the free market works as a powerful self-regulating mechanism of capitalist development, efficiently assigning resources and returns to diverse factors of production (land, labour, capital), and leading to general prosperity, the increased wealth of all nations, has spectacularly failed, requiring of the ideologues and architects of the capitalist system heroic efforts to rescue capitalism from itself. These efforts entail an intensive ideological struggle — to sell the idea of globalization as the only way to the future, development as the solution to underdevelopment and poverty, and the mobility of labour in the global economy as a mechanism of development.

Construction of an agency of change. The workings of the world capitalist system in the form of monopoly capital and at the level of development and migration have created a world in which the lion's share of the social product — the wealth of nations — are appropriated by a small elite group within the international capitalist class, or the global ruling class. In this world, and a system geared to a very uneven world development of the forces of production, labour migrants play a very important role, not only in unwittingly ensuring the expansion of capital (as a lever of capital accumulation) and the survival of the system, but in the formation of a new global proletariat. Whether this proletariat can be turned against the capitalist system in each country where they constitute a vital part of the working class is an open question to which there are no answers at the moment. There is no indication that we are anywhere close to the conversion of these labour migrants as a class "in itself" (super-exploited by capital in its global operations) into a "class for itself," fully conscious of its existence as the most exploited, vulnerable and powerless division of the global working class. On the other hand, as Marx and Engels declared in their *Communist Manifesto,* these workers of the world have nothing to lose but their chains.

Notes

1. However, studies by Bateman (2010) suggest that microfinance is inadvisable, serving primarily as a mechanism of local underdevelopment (destroying local economies from below) and capital accumulation on the basis of super-exploitation of the poor and most vulnerable.

2. Of course, capitalism is not the only structural source of conditions and forces that underlie the motivation and the decisions to migrate. Not all natural disasters or political conflicts, or situations to which migration provides a logical or rational response (one of few if not the only option), can be traced back to the workings of the operative economic system — or at least not directly.

3. Elasticity measures the percentage reaction of a dependent variable in a cause/effect analysis to a percentage change in a independent variable. For example, elasticity of -2 means that an increase by 1% provokes a fall of 2%.

References

Agrela, B., and G. Dietz. 2005. "Emergencia de regimenes multinivel y diversificación público-privada de la política de inmigración en España." *Migración y Desarrollo* 4.

Bateman, Milford. 2010. *Why Doesn't Microfinance Work? The Destructive Rise of Local Neoliberalism.* London: Zed Books.

Bendel, P. 2005. "¿Blindando la 'fortaleza europea'? Intereses, valores y cambios jurídicos en la política migratoria de la Unión Europea." *Migración y desarrollo* 4.

Binford, L. 2002. "Remesas y subdesarrollo en México." *Relaciones* XXIII, 90.

Canales, Alejandro. 2011. "Hacia una visión comprehensiva del nexo entre migración, desarrollo y derechos humanos." *Migración y Desarrollo* 9, 16: 43–79.

Canales, A., and I. Montiel. 2004. "Remesas e inversión productiva en comunidades de alta migración a Estados Unidos. El caso de Teocaltiche, Jalisco." *Migraciones internacionales* 2, 3.

Cordera, Rolando. 2014. "La Gran Transformación del Milagro Mexicano a 20 años del TLCAN." *Revista Problemas del Desarrollo* 180, 46 (enero–marzo).

Delgado Wise, R., H. Márquez and H. Rodríguez. 2004. "Organizaciones transnacionales de migrantes y desarrollo regional en Zacatecas." *Migraciones internacionales* 2, 4.

Delgado Wise, R., and H. Rodríguez. 2001. "The Emergence of Collective Migrants and Their Role in Mexico's Local and Regional Development." *Canadian Journal of Development Studies* XXII, 3.

Durand, Jorge. 1994. *Más allá de la línea: patrones migratorios entre México y Estados Unidos.* Mexico City: CNCA.

García Zamora, Rodolfo. 2003. *Migración, remesas y desarrollo. Los retos de las organizaciones migrantes mexicanas en Estados Unidos.* Mexico City: Doctorado en Estudios del Desarrollo.

Goldring, L. 1996. "Blurring Borders: Constructing Transnational Community in the Process of Mexico–U.S. Migration." *Research in Community Sociology* 1.

Gosh, Bimal. 2007. "The Global Financial and Economic Crisis and Migration Governance." *Global Governance* 16, 3: 317–21.

Guarnizo, L.E. 2003. "The Economics of Transnational Living." *International Migration Review* 37, 3.

Jones, R. 1995. *Ambivalent Journey: U.S. Migration and Economic Mobility in North-Central Mexico.* Tucson: University of Arizona Press.

Kapur, Devesh. 2004. "Remittances: The New Development Mantra?" G-21 Discussion Paper No. 29, April. UNCTAD.

Lapper, R. 2006. *Call for Caution Over Migrant's Cash.* London: Financial Times. <http://www.ft.com/home/uk>.

Massey, D., and E. Parrado. 1998. "International Migration and Business Formation in Mexico." *Social Science Quarterly* 1, 79.

Mines, R. 1981. *Developing a Community Tradition of Migration to the United States: A Field Study in Rural Zacatecas, Mexico, and California*

Settlement Areas. La Jolla: Program in U.S.–Mexican Studies, University of California, San Diego.

Moctezuma, M. 2005. "Morfología y desarrollo de las asociaciones de migrantes mexicanos en Estados Unidos. Un sujeto social y político extraterritorial." *Migración y desarrollo* 5.

____. 2000. "La organización de los migrantes zacatecanos en Estados Unidos." *Cuadernos Agrarios* 19–20.

____. 1999. "Redes sociales, comunidades filiales, familias y clubes de migrantes. El circuito migrante Sain Alto, Zac-Oakland, Ca." PhD dissertation, El Colegio de la Frontera Norte, Tijuana.

Orozco, M. 2003. *Worker Remittances in an International Scope.* Washington: Inter-American Dialogue.

Passel, Jeffrey, and D'Vera Cohn. 2014. "Unauthorized Immigrant Totals Rise in 7 States, Fall in 14. Decline in Those from Mexico Fuels Most State Decreases." Pew Research Hispanic Trends Project. <http://www.pewhispanic.org/2014/11/18/unauthorized-immigrant-totals-rise-in-7-states-fall-in-14/>.

Portes, A., C. Escobar and A. Walton. 2006. "Organizaciones transnacionales de inmigrantes y desarrollo. Un estudio comparative." *Migración y desarrollo* 6.

Ratha, D. 2003. "Workers' Remittances: An Important and Stable Source of External Development Finance." In World Bank. *Global Development Finance 2003: Striving for Stability in Development Finance.* Washington: World Bank.

Reichert, J. 1981. "The Migration Syndrome: Seasonal U.S. Wage Labor and Rural Development in Central Mexico." *Human Organization* 1, 40.

Roldán, Genoveva (ed.). 2013. *La globalización del subdesarrollo en el mundo del trabajo.* Mexico: UNAM-Instituto de Investigaciones Económicas.

Smith, R. 1998. "Transnational Localities: Community Technology and the Politics of Membership Within the Context of Mexico and U.S. Migration." *Comparative Urban and Community Research* 6.

Stuart, J., and M. Kearney. 1981. "Causes and Effects of Agricultural Labor Migration from the Mixteca of Oaxaca to California." *Working Paper in U.S.-Mexican Studies* 28.

Torres, F. 2000. "Uso productivo de las remesas en México, Centroamérica y República Dominicana. Experiencias recientes." Paper presented at Simposio sobre Migración Internacional en las Américas, Organización Internacional para las Migraciones/Comisión Económica para América Latina y el Caribe, San José de Costa Rica, September 4–6.

UNDP (United Nations Development Programme). 2007. *Human Development Report 2007: Human Development and Climate Change.* New York: United Nations Development Programme.

Wiest, R. 1984. "External Dependency and the Perpetuation of Temporary Migration to the United States." In R. Jones (ed.), *Patterns of Undocumented Migration: Mexico and the United States.* Totowa: Rowman & Allanheld.

World Bank. 2014. "Migration and Remittances: Recent Developments and Outlook." *Migration and Development Brief* 23, Migration and Remittances Team, Development Prospects Group. Washington, DC: World Bank. <http://siteresources.worldbank.org/INTPROSPECTS/Resources/3349341288990760745/MigrationandDevelopmentBrief23.pdf>.

Index